CIVIL DISOBEDIENCE
IN ANTIQUITY

TO ALAN AND
CYNTHIA : AND
CALUM AND
NORMA

CIVIL DISOBEDIENCE
IN ANTIQUITY

DAVID DAUBE

Edinburgh, at the
University
Press

◆

© David Daube 1972
EDINBURGH UNIVERSITY PRESS
22 George Square, Edinburgh

ISBN 0 85224 231 X

North America
Aldine · Atherton, Inc.
529 South Wabash Avenue, Chicago

Library of Congress
Catalog Card Number 72-90787

Printed in Great Britain by
W & J Mackay Limited, Chatham

CONTENTS

PREFACE

This is a series of lectures.[1] The choice of material was dictated by a combination of two considerations: what would appeal to my audience ?, and in what field could I think of notable cases ?

I regret the absence of several topics. Two of them are civil disobedience of political minorities and civil disobedience of poets and playwrights. To do them justice I should have had to enter fully into the thorny subjects of treason, freedom of speech and libel—too thorny for me at this stage.

Para-civil disobedience is another province I should have liked to explore: on the one hand, the conscientious breaking of rules of a smaller group, not the state, and on the other, conscientious illegality on the part of the authorities.

The gadfly has its proper place in the former area. Socrates played the part, but he was held to be flouting the laws of the state. Antisthenes, founder of the Cynics, adopted a similar manner, as did Antisthenes's disciple Diogenes, but they were luckier. Antisthenes recommended to his fellow-citizens to pass a law that asses were horses. To the objection that this was absurd, he retorted: 'But we have just appointed so-and-so and so-and-so to be our generals'.[2] It is commoner to find such a tease in a club, on a university faculty or the like.

Two Talmudic sages are good illustrations. Rabbi Jose ben Taddai, around AD 100, by means of exegetical deductions then in fashion at the Jabneh academy proved that you may not marry a woman whose mother's marriage is still on. The President placed him under a ban.[3] Some two hundred years later, Rabbi Jeremiah was expelled from the Tiberias academy. His colleagues

---

[1] Messenger Lectures, delivered at Cornell University, October 19–21 and 26–28, 1971.
[2] Diogenes Laertius 6.8; see Daube, *Natural Law Forum*, **12**, 1967, pp. 5f.
[3] Derek Eretz Rabba 1; see Daube, *Jewish J. Sociol.*, **3**, 1961, pp. 18f.

had arrived at the conclusion that a pigeon found within fifty cubits from a cote belonged to the owner of the cote, beyond fifty cubits to the finder. He asked: 'What if one foot is within fifty cubits and the other beyond?'[1] Another time he dealt with the doctrine that ritual slaughter of animals was required only from the moment the Israelites occupied Canaan. He enquired: 'What were they to do with meat that they had left over from the desert?'[2] The Pharisaic dogma of bodily resurrection called forth many a question designed solely to upset orderly study and preaching.[3] Queen Cleopatra is alleged to have been curious whether the dead would rise clothed or naked.[4] The Sadducees are credited with a frivolous conundrum in the Synoptic Gospels.[5]

A familiar modern variety of this type of disobedience is the filibuster, the obstruction of parliamentary proceedings by an interminable speech.[6]

Law-breaking by the authorities, with a view to safeguarding supreme values, is as old and diversified as civil disobedience proper; and, naturally given the normal power distribution, incomparably more successful. Unjustified harassment and incarceration in the interest of general welfare occur from the dawn of history down to this day. When Supreme Court nominee Rehnquist was questioned as to his opinion of the mass arrests on Washington May Day, he replied that he was not close enough to judge, but 'the fact that there was not a serious injury,

---

[1] Babylonian Baba Bathra 23b.
[2] Babylonian Hullin 17a. Both puzzles concern borderline cases; the first a spatial one, the second a temporal one. A third puzzle posed by him concerns a numerical one, but on that occasion he does not seem to have been subversive. It had been decided that for a sin to be committed in public the presence of ten Jews is required. Jeremiah asked: 'What if there are nine Jews and one Gentile?' Babylonian Sanhedrin 74b.
[3] The rabbis spoke of 'questions of *buruth*, vulgarity'; see Daube, *New Testament Studies*, 5, 1959, pp. 180ff.
[4] Babylonian Sanhedrin 90b.
[5] Matthew 22.23ff., Mark 12.18ff., Luke 20.27ff.
[6] The earliest use of the word in this sense recorded in the *Oxford English Dictionary* (4, 1933, p. 213) is 1882, but it is considerably older. On the other hand, the *Dictionary of American English* (2, 1940, p. 970), following Thornton, *An American Glossary* (1, 1912, p. 315), dates this application from 1853—too soon. In the source quoted, *Congressional Globe*, January 3, 1853, the meaning in question is not yet reached. It first appears in print in the *Congressional Globe*, May 21, 1858, p. 2293.

there was no loss of life, and the Federal government was kept open is quite a significant accomplishment . . . If this could be done without arresting anybody who should not have been arrested that would be even better'.[1]

Again, mature legal systems contain provisions allowing the suspension in an emergency of certain rights of the citizenry. In Republican Rome the appointment of a dictator or the granting of extraordinary powers to the consuls by the *senatusconsultum ultimum* did the trick. But already at a far earlier stage of juris-prudential development, long before such measures are sanctioned by the constitution, many a government with its back to the wall will defend itself by hook or crook; and even nowadays, when those special clauses are invoked, it is often a thinly disguised *Putsch*. Mommsen, with his usual sturdy commonsense, opens his discussion of martial law at Rome with the dictum: 'Necessity is governed by the rules of self-help'.[2]

The situations so far mentioned often involve violence or a threat of violence. There are others essentially civil. A young king, fired by romantic visions, may madly exceed the legitimate budget in order to build castles and sponsor opera.[3] The rise of equity, both at Rome and in other states, can be viewed as to some extent an exercise in defiance of the established order. For England, Sir Edward Coke would certainly have agreed. It all depends, of course, which side you consider to be authentic; in 1616 the privy council found him to have wrongfully interfered with the court of chancery. As for Roman equity, the element of contemptuous rejection of the strict law is readily traceable: a party who wished the latter to be inapplicable to a transaction would say, 'fraud and the strict law shall be excluded'.[4]

A recent article by the brothers Mortimer and Sanford Kadish is entitled 'Justified Rule Departures by Officials'.[5] It deals with such problems as selective law enforcement by police or prosecutor, or acquittal by a jury in the teeth of law and facts. The

---

[1] See *San Francisco Chronicle* of 4 November 1972, p. 26.
[2] Mommsen, *Römisches Staatsrecht*, 3, pt. 2, 1888, p. 1240.
[3] *Das ist Herr Ludwig von Bayerland: Heines sämtliche Werke*, ed. Elster, 2, p. 169.
[4] *Dolus malus abesto et ius civile*; see Bruns, *Fontes Iuris Romani Antiqui*, 1, 7th ed. by Gradenwitz, 1909, p. 340. Sometimes they exclude 'fraud and the expert in strict law', *dolus malus et iurisconsultus*.
[5] *California Law Rev.*, 59, 1971, pp. 905 ff.

analysis is brilliant. Yet it does remain possible to look at the matter in a more pedestrian way, maybe even with a little emotional inexactitude, and, for example, as far as the jury is concerned, to admit some truth in Dean Pound's statement which they quote:[1] 'Jury lawlessness is the great corrective of law in its actual administration'.

I am grateful to my Cornell friends who invited me to deliver these lectures and made me welcome. My warm thanks are due to Professor Reuven Yaron of Jerusalem for reading and commenting on the entire series, and to Professor Peter Stein of Cambridge for reading and commenting on parts of it. My Secretary, Mrs Nancy Siegel, has been immensely helpful. Archie Turnbull, Secretary to the Edinburgh University Press, once again proved understanding and resourceful; I particularly appreciate his courtesy in having an index prepared. Lastly, I am indebted to the Editor and the Publishers of the *Konstanzer Universitätsreden* for allowing me in the first two lectures to draw heavily on my Inaugural Lecture at Konstanz University, *Gewaltloser Frauenwiderstand im Altertum*.[2]

---

[1] P. 920. The reference is Pound, *American Law Review*, **44**, 1910, pp. 12, 18.
[2] *Konstanzer Universitätsreden*, ed. by Gerhard Hess, no. 47, Druckerei und Verlagsanstalt Konstanz, 1971.

THE WOMEN OF
THE BIBLE AND GREECE

1

I ought to begin by saying what I mean by civil disobedience of women in antiquity. I guess I may dispense with a definition of women, though I admit that ever since the recent litigation, Corbett vs. Corbett, alias Ashley, in London,[1] I am no longer so certain of my standing in this matter. By antiquity I mean the Jewish-Greek-Hellenistic-Roman world up to the end of Justinian in the sixth century.

It is more difficult to define civil disobedience.[2] I am not concerned with any unfriendly response like a refusal to be taken out, but only with such behaviour as contravenes the law, or at any rate, deep-rooted custom. Furthermore, I exclude purely selfish actions performed in the hope of remaining undetected; for example, theft of a purse inadvertently left behind in the lecture room. I shall confine myself to offences committed openly, maybe by way of demonstration, in a higher cause or a cause thought to be higher. In this sense it would be civil disobedience, say, if a utopian socialist working-woman entered an elegant shop where purses were sold, declared that she had a better claim to one of them than wealthy idlers, and then simply seized the most attractive specimen from the display. Possibly, too, if a lady-colleague of mine, in order to emphasize equal rights, took my right hand and kissed it in Austrian fashion. Helen of Troy committed adultery, but she did it for pleasure, so she does not qualify for this afternoon's discussion.[3] We may contrast with her Ibsen's Nora who, for the sake of her own liberation as well as that of her fellow-sufferers, leaves her husband and children, her doll's home, and embarks on a lonely

---

[1] See *Weekly Law Reports*, 26 June 1970, pp. 1306 ff.
[2] The literature is enormous. A balanced account is given by Rosen, *George Washington Law Rev.*, **37**: **1**, 1968–9, pp. 435 ff.
[3] See, however, below, The Women of Rome, p. 39.

road. There are, of course, borderline cases. Often it will be easier to class an incident if civil is replaced by civic: civic disobedience brings out more clearly that the act is carried out in the name of society (or a part of it) at large.

I am aware that on psychological probing the distinction between vulgar and principled conduct often dissolves. A person may believe or pretend to act from high-mindedness and in reality be quite egotistic. Or he may look an egotist and even proclaim himself one, yet really have the public good at heart. But I shall, on the whole, take the simplistic approach which ancients as well as moderns use in judging these matters—otherwise this survey would just not be possible. Whatever the science of the soul may bring to light, some interest may attach to how the cases in question were in fact dealt with in former times.

As I understand it, civil disobedience presupposes absence of violence; and from this point of view civic would be less appropriate, it sounds less proper, less 'civilised'—civic resistance, I feel, should cover violent action. No doubt a case might be made for treating civil disobedience as no less inclusive. In fact, I shall later on [1] illustrate at some length the precariousness, if we want to trace the history of a conflict, of separating peaceful and violent behaviour. Moreover, let me make it clear that I can think of circumstances in which I would blame no one for resorting to force. Xenophon was optimistic when, in trying to whitewash the memory of Socrates and dissociate him from wild characters like Alcibiades, he asserted that whatever was attainable by violent means at great cost 'was attainable through persuading, without danger and in friendship'.[2] Still, the means employed do matter; so as far as this series is concerned, permit me to confine civil disobedience to non-violence.

Here again we run into complications and border-line possibilities. On the second of February of this year,[3] at the Hastings College of the Law at San Francisco, while Professor Camera was holding a class, some two dozen lady students entered and clamoured in chorus for his dismissal because he had expressed doubts as to the effectiveness of female attorneys in criminal trials. No violence occurred throughout this incident. But

---

[1] See below, The Women of Rome, pp. 34 ff.
[2] *Memorabilia* 1.2.10; cp. below, Prophets and Philosophers, pp. 73f.
[3] See *San Francisco Chronicle*, 3 February 1971, p. 3.

suppose he had expected the trouble and had barricaded the door by means of a table, perhaps with some flower-pots on it, and the students had overthrown the obstacle. Would this have turned the affair into a violent one? Or suppose the ladies had been boxing champions and had surrounded him with threatening gestures. In this particular case it would not have been so serious because Professor Camera is a great footballer. But I have been at demonstrations which, though in the end they passed without bloodshed, yet in spirit and potentiality were anything but gentle.

For the purpose of this course, it may be best to assume non-violence wherever there is no serious danger to life, limb or objects of value. Medea, who slaughtered before Jason's eyes the children she had borne to him, was obviously violent. If you collect mortars, machine-guns, bombs, with a view to intimidating the government, I subsume it under violence, even before any of these weapons have gone off. On the other hand the English suffragette movement at the turn of the century I deem non-violent, although when it went on people thought very differently: you have a look at the press of the time. The worst that happened was a few broken windows, and Miss Pankhurst ended up as a Conservative Member of Parliament.[1] *Tempora mutantur*: what counts as terrorism in one epoch, stratum of society or situation, counts as innocence itself in another. That the boundary is indeterminate cannot be helped. The Mafia has oscillated from its inception between banditry à la Robin Hood and downright criminality, and between non-violent and violent crime.

One more point concerning definition. It is common in definitions of civil disobedience to require that the perpetrator be willing to undergo the punishment prescribed by the law. I daresay the model in the minds of the proponents of this doctrine is Socrates, who willingly drank the hemlock tendered to him. I shall discuss his trial in the lecture on philosophers.[2] For the moment I would say that I do not concur. I shall not quibble— scholars are free to formulate their premises, and I can see a good deal of sense in this stipulation. However, I do not sub-

---

[1] Most English and American encyclopedias find it unnecessary to carry an entry 'suffragettes'. German and French ones do have it: their readers are intrigued by those female British eccentrics. Contrast *Encyclopaedia Britannica* and *Chambers* with *Brockhaus* and *Larousse*.

[2] See below, Prophets and Philosophers, pp. 72 ff.

scribe to it; and a person who, having performed his act of defiance, attempts the very best defence in court, maybe exploits procedural loopholes, or even one who runs away to a neighbouring country, may still, for the purpose of my lectures, be civilly disobedient. He may not, but he may.

I suspect that a motive—not the only one, but still a motive—behind the restriction of the term to the takers-of-the-consequences has to do with the honourable overtone nowadays attaching to it in a wide section of the public. Those who avoid or evade punishment are to be debarred from this honourable category, with effects which are obviously welcome to the authorities. If you joyfully or at least resignedly accept the legal penalty, you indicate your basic recognition of the regime in power.

Precisely the likely existence of this motive in the advocates of the dominant appraisal is a motive for me to decline it and do without the requirement. I am not persuaded that current notions of honourable conduct are thoroughly justifiable. The question is complicated and a proper exploration would lead too far afield. The orthodox attitude has affinity with the admiration we are invited to have for the 'good loser'—a concept manifestly coined by the lucky winner: he has an enormous interest in the other party putting a cheerful face on the outcome, an interest at once material and concerning his psychic well-being. More generally, it is the entire structure called 'the rules of the game' which the prevalent definition seems to support. But again, they are biased. Of course, substantively the same ideals are formulated differently in different cultures and periods: it is mainly in modern England that they are of a sporting nature. (English society has been outstandingly successful in achieving compliance with them.) However expressed, it is remarkable what a huge influence they are throughout history, in all walks of life public and private.[1] However, I cannot dwell on these ramifications.

To recapitulate, this afternoon's subject will be those women of antiquity who, from avowed conviction yet without the employment of destructive means, flouted the prevalent order.

---

[1] Marcuse is resented by some of his critics more where he gives advice as to relatively legal infringements of the rules of the game than where he recommends simple, open unlawfulness.

4

The oldest record in world literature of the spurning of a governmental decree occurs in the Second Book of Moses.[1] Pharaoh ordered the Hebrew midwives to kill all male new-born immediately on delivery. 'But the midwives feared God and did not do as the king of Egypt commanded them, but saved the men children alive'. In passing: this oldest instance of conscientious disobedience concerns a case of genocide.[2] In our context, however, what interests is the absence of violence; the appeal to a higher duty, very clearly expressed—'they feared God and did not as the king commanded them'—and taken up over a thousand years later by Peter and John when they were threatened because they preached the risen Jesus[3] (though, for this case, we must consider also the parallel of Socrates, 'men of Athens, I shall obey the god rather than you'[4]); and, above all, the female sex of the resisters. A woman is the main figure also in the Greek prototype of civil disobedience: Antigone, who, despite King Creon's strict prohibition, buried her brother who had perished as a traitor. Remember that at that time a corpse left unburied was supposed to find no rest. (I say 'at that time', though the belief retains much of its vitality in ours—if to some extent underground.) Again no violence, again appeal to a higher authority: 'Nor did I deem', she affirms in Sophocles' tragedy,[5] 'that thou, a mortal man, couldst override the immutable, unwritten laws of heaven.'

That both cases involve heroines is not accidental, and if this has hitherto been neglected, it proves only that the male, scholarly world had no eyes for it. Women are largely outside the power structure; indeed, on the whole they belong to the oppressed

---

[1] Exodus 1.15ff.

[2] 'Any of the following acts committed with intent to destroy, in whole or in part, a national, ethnical, racial or religious group, as such: (a) Killing members of the group . . .(d) Imposing measures intended to prevent births within the group'. Article II of the Convention of 9 December 1948, on the Prevention and Punishment of the Crime of Genocide, in *United Nations Treaty Series*, **78**, 1961, p. 280.

[3] Acts 4.19, 5.29: 'Whether it be right to hearken unto you more than unto God, judge you . . . We ought to obey God rather than men'. See below, Religious Minorities, pp. 115f.

[4] Plato, *Apology* 17.29 D; cp. 28. 37 E.

[5] Sophocles, *Antigone* 453f. Translation by Storr, *Sophocles* (*Loeb Classical Library*), **1**, 1912, p. 349.

ones of this earth. 'The stronger rules; we must obey this law and others even more grievous', thus counsels Ismene, Antigone's weaker sister.[1] Enmity to tyranny, or better, the ability to manage without falling in with it, to jog along unaffected by it, not bothering about it, is their typical response. It has been said of *A Doll's House*[2] that 'it is not a feminist play. Ibsen was preoccupied with the struggle between society and the individual, and he chose a woman as his protagonist because he knew that, on the whole, women were more likely to take a personal view of life than men'. Feminist or not, Ibsen is conscious of the trait I am pointing to; so is his biographer from whom I have quoted; so, indeed, is King Creon, only he does not like it. 'She ruins states', Sophocles represents him as complaining,[3] 'she dissipates the host, while discipline preserves the ordered ranks; therefore we must maintain authority and yield no tittle to a woman's will.' When we consider, furthermore, that women have neither the training nor the weapons for physical power struggle, the appropriateness of non-violent resistance becomes even clearer.

The two narratives of the midwives and Antigone are totally independent of one another; not a trace of mutual influence. The common insight they offer is all the weightier. Perhaps I should here insert that I may leave it open whether the events are historical, legendary, or partly this and partly that. They do provide evidence of the role which antiquity attributed to women.

My interpretation is supported by another common feature of the two incidents so widely separated in time, space and cultural background. The actions defying the despot are elementary loving offices: assistance at birth and burial. Women are more closely in touch with becoming and dying than men, hence are more inclined to furtherance and saving of life and humanity and less to destruction and cruelty. 'My nature', exclaims Antigone 'is for mutual love, not hate'.[4] How motherly the poet imagines

---

[1] *Antigone* 63f. (Storr, p. 319: 'The stronger rules; we must obey his orders, these or worse'.)

[2] See Roberts, *Encyclopaedia Britannica*, 12, 1953, p. 38.

[3] *Antigone* 674ff. (Storr, p. 367). Cp. 'No woman shall be master while I live', 525 (Storr, p. 355); 'Son, be warned and let no woman fool away thy wits', 648f. (Storr, p. 365); 'O heart corrupt, a woman's minion thou', 746 (Storr, p. 373); 'A woman's servant thou, do not cajole me', 756 (Storr, p. 373: 'Play not the spaniel, thou a woman's slave').

[4] *Antigone* 523 (Storr, p. 355). Cp. 'To die and rest — two lovers side by side', 73 (Storr, p. 321: 'To die, to rest—sister and brother linked in love's embrace').

her loyalty to her brother to be, and how close it is, therefore, to
the attitude of the midwives, is shown by the description of her
sorrow as she discovers that the soil she had placed on her dead
brother has been removed again. 'There stood this maid, a
piercing cry she uttered, sad and shrill, as when the mother bird
beholds her nest robbed of its nestlings.'[1] Terrible that, precisely for this caring, the king orders her to be dragged to her
death, young, unwedded and childless.[2] His reply to her creed I
have just quoted, 'My nature is for mutual love, not hate', is:
'Die, then, and love the dead, if love thou must; no woman shall
be master while I live.'[3] Senseless male pride drives him to
decisions which in the end result in his being left in tomb-like
desolation.[4]

Antigone is famous, the midwives are not. I am hardly mis-
taken in assuming that, prior to this lecture, of ten persons in
this hall familiar with Antigone, one only remembered the
midwives. The reason is that while Antigone stood by her
deed, the midwives denied theirs. 'The king of Egypt called
for the midwives and said unto them, Why have you done this
thing and have saved the men-children alive? And the midwives replied, Because the Hebrew women are not as the
Egyptian ones; they are lively and are delivered before the midwives visit them'.[5] So they told the king a fib, they had nothing
to do with the birth of these children at all. The arrested
Antigone, when asked by Creon: 'Wast thou acquainted with the
interdict?', answers arrogantly: 'I knew, all knew; how should
I fail to know?'[6] This is the posture our teachers recommended
to our fantasy. Had she answered instead: 'I beg your pardon, I

---

[1] *Antigone* 423 ff. (Storr, p. 347). Her cry, however, also constitutes
a request to the gods for vengeance; the text goes on, 427 f., 'and cursed
the ruffians who had done this deed' (Storr, p. 347). See the discussion
by my brother Benjamin Daube, *Zu den Rechtsproblemen in Aischylos'
Agamemnon*, pp. 99 ff.
[2] 'And now he has me dragged by brutal hands, a bride unwed, amerced
of marriage-joy and marriage-bed and joys of motherhood, by friends
deserted to a living grave', *Antigone* 916 ff. (Storr, p. 385: 'And now he
drags me like a criminal, a bride unwed . . .').
[3] *Antigone* 524 f. (Storr, p. 355). The concluding portion has already
been cited above, p. 6, n. 3.
[4] 'Lead me hence, a less than nothing', *Antigone* 1321 f. (Storr, p. 417).
[5] Exodus 1.18 f. According to a rabbinic suggestion we ought to render
not 'they are lively', but 'they are animals': Exodus Rabba 1 ad loc.
[6] *Antigone* 448 f. (Storr, p. 349).

7

had not heard of it', not much would have happened to her[1] and you would remember her as little as you remember the midwives. Strictly speaking, the latter did not practice civil disobedience according to the definition I laid down at the beginning. That, you may recall, requires openness, publicity. On the other hand, they did not enjoy the protection of absolute, safe secrecy: their conduct was of course widely known, at least among their fellow Jewesses, so that they had constantly to reckon with detection and execution—for they could not hope for mercy. We might compare those Mexican priests who, in the years following 1926, conducted schools contrary to the constitution.

How are we to explain this difference—Antigone's insistence on being called to account, the shrewd escape of the midwives ? Antigone knows that her confrontation, even though it may mean her ruin, will not be in vain. Not only does retribution quickly catch up with the tyrant in that his own son, Antigone's fiancé, and his wife both commit suicide. Not only does he recognize and repent his overweening mistake, if too late. What is of decisive importance is that her unflinching firmness shakes the entire foundation of arbitrary government. To this day her voice is feared by any usurper whose position is in the least endangered.

There are additional factors: her membership of the nobility —pride is a traditional aristocratic virtue—and indeed her personal character. She is both extraordinarily ambitious[2] and desirous of dying. She is a murderee; she does want to be a victim (a wish which does not prevent her from, in the end, being profoundly aware of the questionability and terror of the way she has chosen[3]). 'How sweet to die', she says:[4] and

---

[1] On this kind of ignorance as an excuse, see my article in *Texte und Untersuchungen zur Geschichte der altchristlichen Literatur*, **79**, 1961, p. 61.

[2] 'And yet how otherwise had I achieved a name so glorious ?', *Antigone* 502f. (Storr, p. 353). In this connection, attention should be paid also to her vehement opposition to the innocent Ismene's attempt to be found guilty together with her, 536ff.

[3] *Antigone* 818ff.

[4] *Antigone* 72 (Storr, p. 321). Cp. 'The worst that can befall is but to die an honourable death', 96f. (Storr, p. 323); 'if death is thereby hastened, I shall count it gain', 461f. (Storr, p. 349); 'why dally then ?', 499 (Storr, p. 353): 'thou livest while my soul died long ago', 559f. (Storr, p. 359: 'thou livest, I died long ago').

8

immured in a rock-hewn chamber to perish there, she hastens her death by hanging herself.[1] I would not have allowed her to drive me, though I am fond of lifts. These qualities are hardly surprising in one who definitely came from a broken family: her father was Oedipus, her mother Jocasta, Oedipus' mother and wife.[2] (Just fancy her analyst's reaction in the first session when he asked her: 'Now tell me a little about your parents', and she started: 'Well, my father was Oedipus'.) Here also lies the explanation of her indifference to the disaster her conduct inflicts on innocent by-standers, so to speak—her fiancé, for example. It is a general rule: the more high-minded, the more inconsiderate.[3]

By contrast, there is not the remotest chance of breaching the absolutism of the Pharaohnic regime. Nor are the midwives representatives of an elevated stratum where concealment is despicable; they belong to the common folk. Above all, if they confessed, they would deprive themselves of all possibility of further saving activity.[4] Their lie enables them to carry on their good work unmolested—a consideration which has no place in the case of Antigone. As Ecclesiastes has it (or shall I say, Judy Collins ?):[5] 'To everything there is a season—a time to rend and a time to sew, a time to keep silence and a time to speak.' Whoever is forced to live under a regime of terror, and also whoever wishes to understand those under such a regime, might learn a good deal from the antithesis of Antigone and the midwives.

In Jewish ethics, and to a certain degree in Christian ethics, too, unnecessary provocation of the oppressor is regarded as of dubious value. There are indeed situations where it is not

---

[1] *Antigone* 1221f.
[2] In the *Oedipus at Colonus* (written long after *Antigone*), Antigone loyally acts as her exiled father's guide during his wanderings as a blind beggar. There are strong ties of affection between her and her brother. He has a foreboding of his disastrous fate and begs her to procure him a burial.
[3] The Russian choir at Freiburg, in my time, had on its programme that great song celebrating Stenka Rasin, head of a Cossack rebellion, who, in order to prove to his followers that his mistress, however beautiful, would not make him forgetful of his duty, threw her into the Volga.
[4] The Egyptian king's bitter determination comes out in the edict which he issues now that his plan to use the midwives has failed: the entire population is now commanded to drown any male Hebrew new-born. Exodus 1.22.
[5] 3.1, 7.

9

enough to do the right thing: you must testify to it whatever the consequences. But such radicalism is called for only on the rarest occasions. 'It is not in the nature of man to destroy himself', the Midrash remarks,[1] and Thomas More did not come out before his judges with all his opinions. He was resolved not to deny his faith even should it cost him his life: this would be martyrdom imposed on him by God. But to throw himself into the arms of martyrdom by careless, uncalled-for utterances, he considered presumptuous.[2] My impression is that a considerable portion of the youth of today is sceptical about heroic gestures, and prefers to evade stupid rules and orders quietly, thoughtfully, purposefully, but as far as possible without being hurt. I shall come back to this in my discussion of Socrates' refusal to escape execution.[3]

3

With the story of the midwives we may compare the widespread theme of the rescue of a baby exposed by parents to be destroyed by starvation or wild beasts. In numerous legends a servant commissioned to place the baby in a remote spot, or someone who comes upon it there, takes pity on it and brings it up. Usually the motivation is the simple quality of mercy rather than conviction that the saving of the little one is a higher duty. Even an animal may step in: Romulus and Remus, exposed in the woods, were suckled by a wolf until they were discovered and taken home by a shepherd.

As usual Shakespeare is extremely subtle in his treatment of a problematic situation. In *The Winter's Tale* the king mistakenly believes his new-born daughter to be conceived in adultery. He orders his minister to have her burned that instant. The minister at considerable risk dissuades the king. In the end, the latter decides to make fate the arbiter, though in a way likely to mean death to the child: the minister is to expose her in a deserted place abroad. With a heavy heart he complies and takes her to a forest in Bohemia. Presently a bear comes along, but instead of devouring the baby, he goes for the minister, whereas the baby is eventually saved by a kind soul that finds her.

[1] Genesis Rabba 82 on Genesis 35.17. See Daube, *Theology*, 72, 1969, pp. 291 ff.
[2] See Hollis, *Thomas More*, 1934, p. 231, and Chambers, *Thomas More*, 1935, p. 339.
[3] See below, Prophets and Philosophers, pp. 75 ff.

So Shakespeare makes the minister pay with his life for his action: however hard-pressed, he should not have executed the order. Yet retribution is exacted not by human hand but by heaven. No fellow-man would have had the right to judge in this matter. The minister is condemned by himself—in a dream in which the queen, the wrongly accused mother of the girl, predicts death to him—and by the bear. That it was the presence of a circus at the time near his Globe Theatre which enabled Shakespeare to bring a bear on the stage[1] is typical: he knew how to produce pure gold from anything that came to hand.

Sixteen years later, as the penitent king is reunited with his wife, the minister's widow remarries. She had never wavered in her brave protection of the baby, and the king had contemptuously called her a midwife;[2] yet she had sincerely mourned for her less courageous husband. She now gives her hand to that courtier who had disobeyed the king's order to murder the friend he suspected of being the queen's paramour. Indeed, he had not only not done this bidding, but also revealed the plan to the prospective victim, and abandoned his high position in order to accompany the latter on his flight. The king has long recognized his error and is profoundly grateful to the man whose resistance preserved him from becoming even more fearfully guilty than he was. Here, then, is a case— we shall come across others[3]—where civil disobedience is palpably exercised in the interest of the person disobeyed. The courtier, in disobeying, is truly on the side of his master, whom he saves from irretrievable damnation. The king, during his attack of raving jealousy, is described as 'in rebellion with himself' and he 'will have all that are his so too'.[4] That is to say, it would be the execution of his insensate wishes which would constitute real disloyalty.[5] Many a Quaker believes that, by refusing the call to arms, he is giving his government the truest support.[6]

---

[1] See Quiller-Couch, *The Winter's Tale* (The Works of Shakespeare, ed. Quiller-Couch and Wilson), 1931, p. xx.

[2] 2.3.160.

[3] E.g. the Sabine Women, see below, The Women of Rome, p. 26, or Balaam, see below, Prophets and Philosophers, pp. 65 ff.

[4] 1.2.355 f.

[5] Cp. 2.1.140, where the minister says: 'It is for you we speak'.

[6] A narrow variety of his situation is discussed by Gellius, *Attic Nights* 1.13.

I have remarked on the minister's dilemma in an inquiry into the defence of superior orders.[1] The relation between civil disobedience and this plea is indeed of great interest. Obviously, in many cases the omission of civil disobedience will involve you in a misdeed which you would attempt to justify by invoking a superior order. In Robert Greene's novel *Pandosto*, from which the main plot of *The Winter's Tale* is taken, all these questions are treated interestingly enough, but with less profundity than in Shakespeare.

Antigone's last service to her brother puts one in mind of the touching, brave Biblical figure of Rizpah.[2] When David had succeeded Saul to the throne, the Gibeonites demanded the extradition of seven of Saul's sons for a wrong that their father had done them. David, to whom any survivor of the house of Saul was a potential danger, acceded to the request, and the Gibeonites hanged all seven and left them on the trees. Two of them had been born to Saul by Rizpah. 'And Rizpah took sackcloth and spread it upon the rock and sat from the beginning of the harvest until the rains dropped from heaven, and suffered neither the birds of the air to come upon them by day nor the beasts of the field by night'.[3] David, informed of her action, had the bad conscience that always overcame him when he had got his way by whatever means. He did not victimize her but, on the contrary, gave burial to Saul and Jonathan at least.

Throughout history, authorities have frowned on or even regarded as criminal the decent treatment of the corpse of one destroyed as an enemy; and by decent treatment might be understood ceremonious burial or indeed any burial. Sennacherib, King of Assyria, slew many Jews and threw their bodies behind the city wall: Tobit buried them and when the king learned of it he sought to put him to death for it.[4] According to John, Joseph of Arimathaea, when he gave honourable burial to Jesus, was committing no civil disobedience to Roman rules—he obtained Pilate's permission—though he kept it secret from the Jewish side.[5] In Matthew and Mark, it is a

---

[1] See Daube, *The Defence of Superior Orders in Roman Law*, 1956, p. 6 (repr. in *Law Quarterly Rev.*, **72**, 1956, p. 497).
[2] II Samuel 21.   [3] II Samuel 21.10.   [4] Tobit 1.17ff.
[5] John 19.38. The fear of the Jews is mentioned neither in Matthew 27.58 nor in Mark 15.33 nor in Luke 23.52. Mark 15.43 suggests that Joseph's request was a prima facie affront to the Romans: 'he dared to go in to Pilate and crave the body'.

woman who, by anticipation, anoints his body for his funeral while he is still alive;[1] and in Mark and Luke, it is women who come to his grave in order to anoint his body—but by this time he is risen.[2] After Nero's funeral, Suetonius tells us,[3] 'his nurses Ecloge and Alexandria, together with his concubine Acte, deposited his ashes'.

4

A very archaic instance of civil disobedience is preserved in the cycle dealing with Jacob's progeny. The social structure out of which it springs is so alien from anything today that this very strangeness may render it interesting. I am referring to the narrative of Judah and Tamar.[4] Judah had three sons. The first-born married Tamar but he died early. According to the custom of the time the second one took over: Tamar could not have married outside Judah's family, certainly not while other sons were available, and she had a right to have children. However, the second son also died; the circumstances of his death are interesting but I shall not here go into them. I have discussed them elsewhere.[5]

Judah now is unwilling to risk his third son with Tamar and she is left neglected. She disguises herself as a harlot and brings it about that Judah himself has intercourse with her. He does not, of course, know who she is. Some time later, as she becomes pregnant, Judah, who thinks she has given herself to some illicit pleasure, sentences her to death. But she produces evidence that he is the father of the child. He acknowledges his wrong and her justification, and she is re-accepted into the family in an honourable position. It is indeed from this child (or rather, from one of the twins she bears) that in course of time Joseph, husband of Jesus' mother, descends.[6]

Formally, technically, Tamar, of course, commits an extremely deviant action but she does so convinced that she has a right to insist on being given a child and all the privileges that this motherhood implies. In the history of women's rights in

---

[1] Matthew 26.12, Mark 14.8.
[2] Mark 16.1 ff., Luke 24.1 ff. For more details of the treatment of Jesus' corpse, see Daube, *The New Testament and Rabbinic Judaism*, 1956, pp. 310 ff.
[3] *Lives of the Caesars*, Nero 50.   [4] Genesis 38.
[5] *Juridical Rev.*, **62**, 1950, pp. 71 ff.; see also *Orita*, **3**, 1969, pp. 35 f.
[6] Matthew 1.3, Luke 3.33.

the ancient Hebrew family, this story is significant. It was very hard for a woman, if her husband died before a son was born, to safeguard a tolerable position. She was dependent on the husband's brother or some other near relation perhaps taking her. But the first child from that union would count as a child of the deceased person, which meant that the deceased person's surviving brother or relation would have to share the estate with the newcomer; hence, often, the widow would not be re-married, her brother-in-law and other relations would refuse to have her and thereby to incur considerable material loss. More-over, there might be other circumstances, as in this case, which might stand in the way of a remarriage. In this instance it was the fear that she was a kind of killer, that any husband of hers would die a premature death, which caused Judah to withhold his third son. (We find the same motive much later in the Book of Tobit.[1]) The laws of Deuteronomy [2] in this situation bring some pressure to bear on the surviving brother, in order to make him willing, but even Deuteronomy reckons with the possibility of no success, so that she is left desolate. In the story of Tamar, the widow herself enforces what in the cir-cumstances she considers her due.

Her motives are a mixture of self-interest and righteous battling against degradation. There may well be also a feeling of loyalty to her first dead husband to whom she is determined to procure offspring.[3] At any rate, her audacious mode of self-help is civil disobedience of a kind that was certainly taken note of by the public, and especially the female public, of Hebrew antiquity.

A resistance drama of an entirely different spirit is found in the Book of Esther. The story opens with a magnificent banquet given by the Persian monarch. On the seventh day, slightly drunk, he sends for his beautiful wife, Queen Vashti, to boast with her before his guests. She refuses to appear, and enraged, he convenes the Council of State—composed entirely of men. They fear that unless they take severe measures the example might find imitators among the wives of the princes of the realm. Accordingly, the queen is deposed, and an edict sent out into all corners of the vast empire, stressing that the husband

---

[1] Tobit 3.7 ff.   [2] 25.5 ff.

[3] The widow's charge in Deuteronomy 25.9, if her brother-in-law refuses to marry her, is that he 'will not build up his (dead) brother's house'.

is the lord in the family and that his language be spoken. Thus is the road opened for Esther's accession to the throne.

I cannot here go into the puzzle how the Bible alone of all ancient works comes to include such an impressive recital of the hopeless yet resolute claim of a woman to dignity. We shall see in a subsequent lecture [1] that the Book of Esther generally attaches much importance to a person's standing in public, vis-à-vis his peers, his superiors and his inferiors. Also, this work certainly displays great interest in the role of women: after all, it has a title heroine, Esther. Nevertheless, it is astonishing to find an issue being made of what as a rule in oriental conditions must have been a very minor insult, if any insult at all—a husband's order to his beautiful wife to show herself before his honoured guests. [2]

It might perhaps be thought that I am giving this lady credit for a stance she never aspired to; and that she was merely propelled by a momentary caprice. But it is unlikely that she would risk everything for no good reason. Moreover, the reference to the king's wine-humour strongly indicates that we are to conceive of her as unwilling to suffer humiliation. In any case, what is indisputable is that—from whatever motive—she will not comply with a husband's arbitrary summons.

The Book evidently condemns her conduct. She is never heard of again, and we are given to understand that by a more accommodating behaviour, such as that adopted by her successor Esther, in effect a wife can achieve important objects, so it is unwise, vain, to stand too much on outward signs. A man, at least in certain circumstances, should uphold his state. Mordecai, we shall see when we come to discuss religious minorities, does not bow before Haman and, after initial difficulties, he triumphs. For a woman, it is preferable to give in in these matters, and thereby win a position of influence and advantage.

As a matter of fact, the Book of Esther depicts three types of women. One is Queen Vashti, who determines to guard her female and royal dignity and loses her crown. In a way, this is mild treatment, so there is some sympathy for her. She might

---

[1] Below, Religious Minorities, pp. 87 ff.
[2] The rabbis hit on a naughty interpretation of the text which does make the order shameless. The queen was to appear, the text says (1.11) 'with the crown royal'. According to the Targum and Esther Rabba 2 ad loc., this means that she was to appear with nothing but the crown royal.

have been put to death (as she is indeed in a later legend[1]); instead, she is merely dismissed. Still, the Bible does disapprove of this type. The second type is Haman's, the villain's, wife, who simply falls in in the crudest fashion with anything her husband does and says. She is ruined together with him. The type that is celebrated is, of course, the third: Esther, who is not concerned with show, who while it seems useful conceals her antecedents, who does everything to gain her royal husband's favour, but who, by her immense intelligence, her subtle playing off of one person against another, her capacity to wait and her exact timing and choosing the right moment to speak out, gains all she wants. That she applies these talents in a worthy cause goes without saying. Moreover, she never ceases to listen to the counsel of her cousin Mordecai who adopted her as she became an orphan: the narrator emphasizes her continued submissiveness to him even after her marriage.[2]

Let me draw your attention to a strange detail. In ancient literature we hear astonishingly little about the complications arising in a bilingual marriage, say, in a Greek-Persian or a Roman-British one. The edict just mentioned is one of the earliest references to them.[3] It assigns priority to the language of the husband which implies that, if things were left unregulated, on the whole, the wife's language would prevail in the house. Generally, a law is needed where, without it, the opposite would be the rule. The edict reckons with the wife's language naturally preponderating. That is still so today provided the husband's does not represent a higher, more advantageous cultural level.[4]

---

[1] Esther Rabba 3 on Esther 1.21, 4 on 2.1.   [2] Esther 2.20.

[3] The text of Esther 1.22 is not without some difficulty, but there is little doubt as to its meaning.

[4] Hence the expression 'mother tongue'. In Nehemiah 13.24 it is noticed with horror that the children from marriages with foreign wives—marriages to be condemned anyhow—do not speak Hebrew. Both the mothers and the children are cast out. The Greek concubines of the Pelasgians in Herodotus 6.138 brought up their children in Greek: they of course looked on their civilization as vastly superior to the Pelasgian. The Pelasgians killed both the mothers and the children. Ausonius was enchanted by his little German girl's barbarian name Bissula (poem 4, 4f.). She had, however, acquired Latin (poem 3, 10f.). One way of getting over a beloved's ignorance of one's language is indicated by Heine in his poem Wechsel celebrating a new French girl-friend (*Heines sämtliche Werke*, ed. Elster, I, p. 280): *Sie behauptet, sie verstünde Gar kein Deutsch—ich glaub' es nicht.*

5

I come now to the *Lysistrata*, a comedy by Aristophanes, which equals Shakespeare's *Tempest* in profundity and excels it in ambiguity, or perhaps in unambiguity. As the war between Athens and Sparta goes on endlessly and senselessly, the women of the two cities conspire to abstain from intercourse both with husbands and friends until peace is concluded. (At Birmingham in England, wives of striking motor car workers have recently been reported[1] to have shut out their husbands from the bedrooms in order to make them disgruntled and return to the factories—not quite the same thing.) Moreover, the Athenian women occupy the Parthenon, a temple where the public treasury with the war chest is housed, a kind of Fort Knox: the first sit-in in history.

In this revolt, too, exactly as in the cases of the midwives and Antigone, the intention is to protect and rescue human values and to call a halt to barbarous devastation. The dialectic of the situation brings it about that the women prove their love precisely by barring its joys during the war which, while conducive to facile amatory diversion, tramples on the genuine article in three ways: the married women are left behind by their soldiering husbands, the unmarried ones grow up for a lonely existence, and—worst misuse—the sons born and brought up in sweet devotion are being sent to their death.[2] The participants in the action, it should be noted, are all married. Their motherliness prompts them to feel particularly for the young girls condemned to remain single.

The word *sozo*, to save, to bring salvation, which in Greek religiosity often alludes to redemption, occurs quite a few times.[3] The aim, reached only in the play, alas, not in reality, is to free the men—and be it against their stupid will—from the killing they are entangled in,[4] and to unite them in fertile friendship.[5] Significantly, the name of the Spartan female

---

[1] *San Francisco Chronicle* of 7 December 1970, p. 21.
[2] *Lysistrata* 589 ff.   [3] E.g. 41, 497 ff., 525.
[4] 'Whether you like it or not, we'll deliver you'.—'That were a terrible shame, by Demeter'.—'Friend, we must save you'.—'But how if I wish it not?'—'That will but make our resolve the completer', 499 ff. Translation by Rogers, *Aristophanes* (*Loeb Classical Library*), 3, 1946, pp. 49 f.
[5] 'O Artemis, come to join our friendly feasties, to knit our sauls

leader, Lampito, has the same meaning as that of one of the midwives, Shiphra, 'the shining one'; and I trust the militant wing of Women's Lib will not be offended by the fact that in all three cases, the midwives, Antigone, and Lysistrata, the women fight for members of the male sex: for the male new-born, for the slain brother, for the soldiers at the front. Aeschylus, highly admired by Aristophanes, had mentioned as an objection to wars like the Trojan, which had been caused by the abduction of Helen, that 'men die for the sake of women'. Unmistakably behind such a critique lurks a higher ranking of man in comparison with woman.[1] In Aristophanes' comedy, however, the women insist on more rights and on being heard precisely because they can no longer bear the insane slaughter of men by men. Women here try to cause wars to cease.

As their main enemies they regard dried-up old fogies[2] and politicians,[3] both hostile to true, genuine life; the former without a spark, the latter greedy for office and positions. They share Plato's view[4] that lust for wealth and luxury, avarice, is the cause of wars: 'What, is the war for the sake of the silver, then?'—'Yes; and all other disputes that there are. Why is Peisander forever embroiling us ? Why do the rest of our officers feel always a pleasure in strife and disturbances ? Simply to gain an occasion to steal.'[5] The laws produced by these men cannot but be harsh and bitter.[6] The magistrate who opposes the rebels is swathed by them in wreaths and funeral ribbons:[7] that is how they see the ruling clique, mouldering corpses. They look on themselves as equal to men in intelligence and as superior to them in judgement and discrimination between essence and surface lustre.[8] There are certainly values for which one might even go to battle; for example, one might defend

---

thegither an' gie us peace in store an' love for evermore!', 1262 ff. (Rogers, p. 119); 'Call upon Artemis, her brother, Bacchus, Zeus, his queen, the holy witnesses, call them to witness the peace and the harmony, this which divine Aphrodite has made', 1280 ff. (Rogers, p. 121).
[1] See Benjamin Daube op. cit., pp. 84, 139.
[2] 325, 652. This is not entirely a matter of chronology: there are elderly gentlemen who can be trusted. Lysistrata herself says: 'I'm of myself not badly off for brains, and often listening to my father's words and old men's talk, I've not been badly schooled', 1125 ff. (Rogers, p. 109).
[3] 489, 577.
[4] *Phaedo* 66 C ff., *Republic* 2.373 D. See Benjamin Daube op. cit., p. 69.
[5] 489 ff. (Rogers, p. 49).
[6] 324, 703 ff.   [7] 599 ff.   [8] 1124 ff.

Greece against the Persians.[1] The women themselves success-
fully ward off the police who try to eject them from the
Parthenon. 'What did you expect, you fool,' they tease the magistrate who led the attack on them, 'was it unknown to you that
we women, too, can be raging?'[2] But men fight for crude objects
and indeed for the sake of fighting; they love to show themselves in uniform and to boast—not only to the enemy but even
to their most innocent fellow-citizens: 'Troth, 'tis a mighty
ridiculous jest, watching them haggle for shrimps in the market-
place, grimly accoutred with shield and with crest. Lately I
witnessed a captain of cavalry, proudly the while on a charger
he sat, buying an omelet, stowing it all in his cavalry hat. Comes
a Thracian irregular, shaking his dart and his target to boot;
off runs the shop-girl, appalled at the sight of him, down he
sits soldierly, gobbles her fruit'.[3]

The insurrection has two fronts, a private one, in so far as the
individual Athenian or Spartan woman must somehow deal
with her husband or friend, and a public one, where it is
a question of maintaining occupation of the temple and,
ultimately, of enforcing a basic change for the better in the relations between the two cities. As far as the private front is concerned, the women must look as seductive as possible so that
their refusal should hurt all the more. They also agree that if a
man uses force to get his lady into the bedroom, she should hold
fast to the door and any suitable piece of furniture; but if he
starts beating her up she may yield, yet so ill-humouredly that he
will derive little pleasure from the transaction.[4] An extremely
effective way to make clear to a passionate husband what he

---

[1] 1133f. Like Amos in the Old Testament, Lysistrata pronounces her
fellow-countrymen no less culpable than the Spartan enemy: all have
sinned, all ought to make concessions, forgive. However, when it comes
to the barbarians, the Persians, there is a limit even to her love of peace;
cp. Benjamin Daube op. cit., pp. 91ff. See also the next footnote, about
another area blocked out: slavery.
[2] 463ff. (Rogers, p. 45: 'What did the fool expect? Think you we
women feel no thirst for glory?'). Lysistrata is speaking; and one of the
things she says is 'Did you believe you would be coming only upon some
slave maids?' (Rogers: 'Was it to fight with slaves you came?'). Some
of her preaching is reminiscent of the prophets: there is to be brother-
hood between citizens and sojourners, mother city and colonies, rich
and poor, 579ff. Yet slavery continues unchanged. It is no different in
The Female Parliament: see below, p. 21.
[3] 559ff. (Rogers, pp. 57f.).   [4] 149ff.

loses by the strike is shown in a scene[1] which I would not dare to describe to my respectable audience. I must be content with the hint that, compared with what this poor lovelorn chap is being put through, the tortures of Tantalus who, standing in water up to his chin, is eternally thirsty because, as soon as he bends down to drink, the water disappears, and who is eternally starving because the branches full of fruit which touch his forehead are swept away by a wind as soon as he tries to reach them, are mere child's play.

In passing—it is significant that the idea of homosexual activity as a way out does not occur. In fact, except for a brief aside making fun of a rich pederast,[2] that area is not mentioned at all throughout the play.[3] On the whole, homosexuality was confined to a relatively small upper stratum of society, and even there it played the role of champagne, not of *vin ordinaire*. After all, a strike of women would cause much hardship even at North Beach in San Francisco.

On the public front, while things are not entirely peaceful, they are not much worse than in the suffragette years, or in the Berkeley of 1964 when the parties were not yet divided by a wide gulf. *Lysistrata* is a comedy in which there may be neither corpses nor even serious injuries. The women seize the Parthenon by means of a stratagem: some elderly ladies assemble there on the pretence to offer a sacrifice, then they admit all the others, and now the doors are barricaded,[4] so there is no more money for the war. A number of enraged citizens of advanced years (the young ones are at the front) come along with burning oak beams and fire pots in order to smoke out the occupants—a kind of tear gas attack—and if necessary even to drive them out by setting fire to the building. The smoke hurts mainly the attackers, and the fire is prevented by excellent planning and co-operation of the defenders. The men now stand there drenched with water,[5] when at last a magistrate appears with his police. There is a scuffle, but the magistrate's assistants, badly led and not very numerous, have the worst of it.[6] In Berkeley it is generally held that last year's sit-in at Moses Hall was so effectively and smoothly defeated because a

---

[1] 829 ff.
[2] 1092. This and several neighbouring lines are left untranslated by Rogers, p. 105. Too dirty.
[3] See Seel, *Aristophanes oder Versuch über Komödie*, 1960, p. 40.
[4] 175 ff., 240 ff. [5] 254 ff. [6] 424 ff.

huge number of police intervened at the appropriate moment under the most exact instructions. The entire affair is depicted by Aristophanes most convincingly, right into details like the sudden rumour among the citizens that the lady rebels are instigated by men and indeed, by external agents, by Spartans;[1] also the final recognition, after mutual affection and common sense have proved victorious, that it would be a good thing if statesmen conducted their business and negotiations, not when they are sober and therefore petty and suspicious, but when they are a little turned-on.[2]

Some twenty years after the *Lysistrata*, Aristophanes wrote *The Female Parliament*. The theme here is that the women are fed up with the male mismanagement of the city. They disguise themselves as men and early in the morning, long before the bulk of the real men get up, appear in the legislative assembly; they move that the government be handed over to the women and, of course, the motion is carried. The entire city is now being reorganized as one large household, a happy commune, in which there is neither private property nor private marriage. Meals are in common and free, everything is at the disposal of everybody, and there is complete promiscuity—except, indeed, that slavery remains:[3] that was just too anchored an institution and too necessary in the eyes of the free for civilized existence. The constitution is indeed utopian, but again the women are found on the side of life, general joy and advance. Special arrangements are laid down to insure that the freedom in sexual matters will not disadvantage ugly men and women.[4] For example, a presentable young guy, before he spends a night with the lady of his choice, has to be gallant to one not a beauty queen who chooses him. An amusing scene (it would be brutal if performed before a female public, but in Aristophanes' time women did not as a rule attend comedies[5]) reveals the poet's understanding for the ageing woman who is in a harder situation than the ageing man.[6]

---

[1] 619ff. Cp. Cato's insinuation below, The Women of Rome, p. 28.
[2] 1228ff.
[3] 651. Cp. above, p. 19, n. 2.   [4] 614ff.
[5] See Ehrenberg, *The People of Aristophanes*, rev. ed., 1962, pp. 27, 201, 385, *Aristophanes und das Volk von Athen*, transl. from the English by Felten, 1968, pp. 395f.
[6] This fact of life is referred to in so many words in *Lysistrata* 593ff. Cp. also *Plutus* 959ff.

In his recent publication *A Certain World*,[1] W. H. Auden suggests that males are so ridiculously jealous of one another that with modern machinery at their disposal this is now a real threat to the survival of the human race. 'Today our phallic toys have become too dangerous to be tolerated: I see little hope for a peaceful world until men are excluded from the realm of foreign policy altogether and all decisions concerning international relations are reserved for women, preferably married ones.' Auden, a great poet and an excellent classical scholar, is alive to the desperately serious nucleus in Aristophanes' comedy. As for his special confidence in married women, who know what loving means, what children mean, what sorrow means, the conspirators in the *Lysistrata*, we saw,[2] all belong to this category. In *The Female Parliament*, owing to the abolition of binding unions, the distinction between married and unmarried loses its importance. Homosexuality is of as little relevance in the latter comedy as in the former.[3]

---

[1] I quote from McCabe's column in *San Francisco Chronicle*, 8 October 1971, p. 51.   [2] Above, p. 17.   [3] See above, p. 20.

THE WOMEN OF ROME

1

When I started on these lectures, I expected virtually no civil disobedience of women at Rome; and while I was somewhat over-optimistic (or pessimistic?), there are no Roman counterparts of Antigone or Lysistrata, let alone Medea. The reason, however, is not that the Roman women were more femininely docile than the Athenian ones, but on the contrary that they assimilated, identified with, their menfolk's set of values to a higher degree. I mean, of course, the women noticed by the makers of literature, in general, the uppermost class.

Take that early heroine, Lucrece.[1] She was a beautiful noble-woman. In her husband's absence, the son of the overbearing king Tarquin visited her and proposed to her. She declined disgustedly. He threatened to kill her unless she gave in. She remained unmoved. Then he declared that, if she persisted in her refusal, he would slay both her and a slave, place the latter naked by her side and proclaim that he had caught them in adultery. (He would probably have had the right in such circumstances to despatch them on the spot, being a close relation of her husband's;[2] but we need not be too precise about a legend.) On this, she yielded. As soon as he was gone however, she summoned father and husband, informed them of what had happened, exhorted them to vengeance and stabbed herself to death. The affair ended in the abolition of the monarchy.

Here, then, is a woman fighting despotism. Yet for one thing, she acts throughout within the law; it is her ravisher who is

---

[1] Livy 1.58. See Münzer, Pauly-Wissowa, **13**: **2**, 1927, p. 1692. A detail of her suicide not here mentioned is discussed in my *The Linguistics of Suicide* (a lecture delivered at Berkeley in 1970, *Philosophy and Public Affairs*, **1**, 1972, pp. 412f.).

[2] This view is met as early as in Diodorus Siculus 10.20.2. Cp. Appleton, *Revue historique de droit français et étranger*, 4th ser. **3**, 1924, p. 257.

guilty of lawlessness. For another, what is she sacrificing herself for ? In order to set up the most absolute standard of virtue for her sex. 'No unchaste woman shall ever live through the example of Lucrece', are her last words. What does unchastity mean? It means forgetfulness about a husband's exclusive right to his wife. Moreover, even if morally blameless, as she was,[1] a wife defiled should not make her husband put up with what is now devalued property. Her formulation as she tells her husband what has befallen her is significant: 'The print of a strange man is in your bed'. How all-important it is for her to prove herself a faithful stewardess of her lord's estate becomes clear when we reflect that she could have escaped the illicit embrace—if that itself was so unbearable—by letting herself be killed together with a slave. But that would have resulted in her posthumous disgrace as a worthless wife, undeserving her husband's trust. So she submits to the blackmailer and destroys herself. The Biblical Susanna in a similar dilemma chose differently. As an eighteenth-century epigram has it—*Casta Suzanna placet: Lucretia, cede Suzannae. Tu post, ille mori maluit ante scelus.*[2] 'Of all chaste wives, Susanna wins the race. Lucrece, misused, to live refused. Susanna chose to die before the embrace.'

Lucrece would be as unthinkable in ancient Athens as Lysistrata in ancient Rome. Valerius Maximus, writing in the reign of Tiberius, credits her with 'a masculine spirit to which a malevolent error of fortune allotted a female body'.[3] Which does not imply that her story did not greatly impress Greek authors, like Diodorus Siculus of the middle of the last century

---

[1] Augustine, to be sure, wonders (*City of God* 1.19) whether she may not have enjoyed herself a little and, therefore, had a bad conscience. This is reminiscent of Kleist's epigram Die Marquise von O ... (*Heinrich von Kleists sämtliche Werke*, ed. Grisebach, **2**, p. 389): *Dieser Roman ist nicht für dich, meine Tochter. In Ohnmacht ! Schamlose Posse ! Sie hielt, weiss ich, die Augen bloss zu.* 'Not for you, my daughter, this novel. Some fainting! How brazen a story, when all she did was to hold her hands in front of her eyes'.

[2] Quoted by Appleton op. cit., pp. 239, 262, from the *Nouveau Dictionnaire historique*, 1785, s.v. Lucrece. The story of Verginia, which already Livy compares to that of Lucrece (3.44.1), is close to that of Susanna in this respect: appearances are not placed above substance. Verginia's father, as there is no other way out, kills her before she suffers defilement. There are further differences, often neglected, between the two legends.

[3] 6.1.1. *Virilis animus* recurs in 8.3.1 with reference to Maesia, whose achievements I shall advert to presently. See also below, p. 26, n. 1.

B C.[1] Yet the quotation fully accords with my analysis: the Roman women adopted the masculine way of looking at the world, and that is why there was less of that fundamental disobedience.

This entering into the men's scheme of things led to a considerable amount of competition between the sexes. Livy tells us how Coriolanus, about to attack Rome with a superior army, was persuaded by his mother and wife to retreat; and how a temple commemorating the ladies was built. He remarks:[2] 'The men of Rome did not then envy the women what fame belonged to them'. By his time at least, such envy was not to be denied. It is consistent with this picture that, in several areas of the law, the women improved their position without much commotion, by means of dodges; no civil disobedience, just a clever use of existing legal machinery. A well-known example is the device by which it became possible for a woman to obtain an accommodating guardian: by *coemptio* she gave herself as a matter of form to a man who at once made her over to another one designated by her—the latter, on releasing her, would become her guardian.[3]

Apparently, towards the end of the Republic, there was a danger of women taking to advocacy. In general, a woman even in litigation of her own got a male protector, a relation or friend of some influence, to plead before the magistrate.[4] There were, however, exceptions; and one Maesia[5] who, when prosecuted, defended herself in person with notable efficiency has the admiration of Valerius Maximus:[6] she was endowed, like Lucrece, with 'a masculine spirit'. A contemporary of hers, by name of Afrania,[7] upset the apple-cart. Valerius Maximus depicts her as litigious. Moreover, though she could have found men to represent her, she immodestly conducted one case after another herself and, indeed, pestered the authorities a good deal. She would always find some little point to impede the closing of a matter; she would not let go. (Her husband, known only as such, was nicknamed 'Dummy'.[8] Valerius Maximus

---

[1] 10.21. See Münzer op. cit., p. 1694. [2] 2.40 11f. [3] Gaius 1.114f.
[4] See below, pp. 29f, on Valerius Maximus 8.3.3.
[5] See Münzer, Pauly-Wissowa, 14: 1, 1928, p. 282.
[6] 8.3.1—although the introduction to this chapter 8.3 contains a general condemnation of women speaking in public. I shall cite the relevant portion below, p. 31, n. 2.
[7] See Münzer, Pauly-Wissowa, 3, 1899, p. 1589.
[8] *Bucco.* See Münzer, Pauly-Wissowa, 13: 1, 1926, p. 232.

gives the year of her death—'since of such a monster one ought to record the date it perished rather than that it rose up'.) As a preventive measure, a provision was now inserted in the praetor's Edict, excluding women from appearing on behalf of another person.[1] Imperial Rome had women gladiators[2] but no women lawyers: I refrain from citing contemporary analogies.

To be sure, there is no dearth, in the sources, of illustrations of female courage and devotion in a hard, male world; but they do not really qualify as civil disobedience. In its early days Rome was short of women; on the occasion of an intertribal festival, therefore, the bachelors abducted Sabine girls and married them by force. The Sabines invaded Rome, but the brides, by now reconciled to their situation, rushed in between the battling hosts, parted them and induced them to make peace.[3] In so far as this is civil disobedience,[4] it belongs to that kind committed entirely with a view to the welfare of those who are being disobeyed.[5] The first of the kings, Romulus, is credited[6] with naming the thirty *curiae*, city-wards, after these heroines; one is reminded of the cryptic notice in the narrative

---

[1] Valerius Maximus' account is in agreement with Digest 3.1.1.5 (Ulpian 6 ad edictum), and there is no reason for disbelieving it. He mentions yet a third, highly gifted oratress of the late Republic, Hortensia (see Münzer, Pauly-Wissowa, **8: 2**, 1913, pp. 2481f.): an incident in which she figured will be discussed below, pp. 29ff. In D. 3.1.1.5, the part beginning with *ne contra* seems to have suffered interference; see *Index Interpolationum* ad loc. A comparison of its vocabulary with Valerius Maximus yields this result: D. *contra pudicitian*, V.M. *impudentia*; D. *virile officium*, V.M. *virilis animus* (in 8.3.1, concerning Maesia—cp. 6.1.1 which was cited above, p. 24, n. 3); D. *improbissima femina*, V.M. *improbae feminae*; D. *inverecunde*, V.M. *verecundia* (in the introduction to 8.3). Of the two objections to women advocates mentioned in D.3.1.1.5, Lenel, *Zeitschrift der Savigny-Stiftung*, **39**, 1918, *Rom. Abt.*, p. 130, considers the first one, *ne contra-immisceant*, spurious. The Florentine manuscript reads *nec contra*. In view of the *nec* it is possible that this idea was originally interpolated in second place and obtained first place only at a later stage of transmission. However, the *c* may be due to a mere, inadvertent dittography: the following word being *contra*, it was easy for a scribe to write *nec* instead of *ne* by mistake.
[2] See Lecky, *History of European Morals*, **I**, 1902, p. 281.
[3] Livy 1.13.
[4] As we shall see below, p. 29, Lucius Valerius, speaking on behalf of women intruding into the Forum, uses—or misuses—this case as a precedent: Livy 34.5.8.
[5] See above, The Women of the Bible and Greece, p. 11.
[6] Livy 1.13.6f.

about the god-fearing midwives in Egypt:[1] 'Therefore God dealt well with the midwives and made them houses'. Another tale has retained its fascination.[2] It had been arranged between Rome and Alba that a combat between three youths of each city should decide which was to hold dominion over the other. Two of the Romans having succumbed, the remaining one succeeded in despatching all his three opponents. As he returned in triumph, however, his sister, who had been engaged to one of the enemy champions, broke into lamentations and was killed by the infuriated victor. The harsh Roman spirit comes out in the legend culminating, not in an apotheosis of the girl, but in the sparing of the killer's life by popular demand. Again, we hear of women visiting an imprisoned and starving father or mother and, being prevented from bringing them any food, nourishing them with their own milk.[3] I could go on.

2

Two instances of mass civil disobedience on the part of women both involved an invasion of the Forum in order to make an impact there on the course of legislation concerning them. In the first case, in 195 BC, the grievance was restrictions as to dress,[4] in the second, in 42 BC, a special tax.[5] *Au fond*, both times, rich ladies were anxious to preserve, if not increase, their behind-the-scenes influence. Both times they were successful.

A law passed during the second Punic war, when it was essential to husband the fast diminishing resources, imposed limits on female expenditure.[6] A few years after the war its abrogation was moved, but the die-hards would have none of this. The debate went on for days; and, contrary to custom, distinguished matrons in great numbers buttonholed the leading men on their way to the Forum and in the end beleaguered the offices of the two conservative tribunes until these gave up blocking the proposed measure. A reactionary address by Cato and a progressive one by Lucius Valerius (why is he not on Women's Liberation buttons?) supplied by Livy are largely

---

[1] Exodus 1.20f. [2] Livy 1.24ff.
[3] Valerius Maximus 3.4.7, ext. 1, Pliny, *Natural History* 7.36.121.
[4] Livy 34.1ff.
[5] Valerius Maximus 8.3.3, Quintilian 1.1.6, Appian, *Civil Wars* 4.5.32ff.
[6] See my *Roman Law*, 1969, p. 87; on pp. 124ff. I high-light a more general aspect of the sumptuary laws which I shall not here discuss.

fictitious; but for my purpose this matters little — the main thing is that we find here ancient ideas on this incident. One observation at least in the pro-feminine speech seems not far from the truth: that it was the sight of conspicuous foreign women, not falling under the oppressive statute, which goaded their Roman sisters into desperate action. (This motive was pointed out by Lucius Valerius, in reply to Cato's censure of the Roman women for wishing to outdo one another: that was not in their minds, they were aggrieved by the unfair foreign competition.) It was a period of economic and cultural expansion, bringing with it a taste for refinement and luxury. There was a real risk of the men finding truer companionship in an alliance, legitimate or illegitimate, with an elegant, well-dressed foreigner than a dowdy native who could spend only a few dollars a year on a secondhand hat.[1]

Many of Cato's claims are of a perennial nature: that if a woman had anything to say, she should say it in private, to her husband; that even then she should keep off public affairs; that if each husband kept his own wife in order, no large-scale movement could come about; that if women took to secret conventions, the ugliest results, not excluding mass-doing-away with men, might ensue; that their present aggressiveness seemed instigated by male politicians for the latter's ends (a similar suspicion we found entertained by the Athenians in Aristophanes' *Lysistrata*[2]); and that once they started acquiring new rights, they would finish by demanding equality.

Cato called their procedure a sedition and indeed a secession, comparable to the famous withdrawals of the plebeians which compelled the patricians to give in: I shall devote a large part of my final lecture to them. Sedition is the insubordination of a multitude to a magistrate,[3] and secession is one variety of it.[4] The reference to the former might be just tenable; that to the latter is largely rhetoric though supported by the etymology of sedition: *sed-itio*, 'a going away', 'a parting', 'a breaking

---

[1] As for the spirit of that period, see Polybius 31.25.4; cp. Kroll, *Die Kultur der Ciceronischen Zeit*, **2**, 1933, p. 43.

[2] 619 ff.; see above, The Women of the Bible and Greece, p. 21.

[3] See Mommsen, *Römisches Strafrecht*, 1899, p. 562.

[4] *Seditio* is often used of the plebeian withdrawals, e.g. Livy 2.32.1 f., 33.2, 3.50.14, as is the Greek *stasis*, e.g., Dionysius of Halicarnassus 7.13.2, 15.2. More comments on terminology below, Aspirants to Statehood, pp. 143, 145 f.

up'[1]—from this point of view any sedition might be labelled as a secession. Anyhow it was easy for Lucius Valerius to refute the charge, by emphasizing women's helplessness; it was precisely men's enormously powerful position, he submitted, which obliged them to self-restraint. Again, Cato blamed the women for rioting, not with a charitable or religious aim, but in their own petty interest, with a view to pomp and splash. Nothing more natural, rejoined Lucius Valerius: men did the same.

Needless to say, Lucius Valerius no more than Cato disdained specious argumentation. He adduced[2] the brave intervention of the Sabine women, when their fathers and brothers were about to battle their husbands in the centre of the city, as a precedent justifying public action on the part of women and indeed action on the Forum. I mentioned the old legend above.[3] The analogy is manifestly forced.

A quip which Plutarch attributes to Cato[4] may go back to this occasion—what he said to the journalists asking him to comment on the result: 'All other men rule their wives; we rule all other men; and our wives rule us'. One knows the type of men who sigh in this manner about their subjection to women. Still, he does deserve credit for showing some humour when the women got the better of him.

Let us note that in Livy's view the matter which so inflamed the passions was in itself really trivial:[5] a distinctly male approach.

3

Some one-hundred-and-fifty years later, the worm turned again. As a rule, women were not then taxed.[6] The triumvirs Marc Antony, Octavian and Lepidus, however, imposed a huge levy (with nasty threats in case of evasion) on fourteen hundred who were (a) exceptionally wealthy and (b) relations of the proscribed enemies of the triumvirs. In normal times, their cause would have been taken up by a male protector; in the circumstances, no man dared come forward;[7] they had to act

---

[1] Cp. Cicero, *de Re Publica* 6.1.1.   [2] Livy 34.5.8.   [3] See pp. 26f.
[4] More precisely, of which he says that Cato borrowed it from Themistocles: Cato Maior 8.2f., Themistocles 18.5. See Pastorino, *Plutarco, Detti e vita di Catone Maggiore*, 1951, p. 132.   [5] 34.1.3: *res parva dictu.*
[6] See Mommsen, *Römisches Staatsrecht*, 3, pt. 1, 1887, pp. 236f.
[7] Valerius Maximus: *nec quicquam virorum patrocinium eis accommodare auderet.*

themselves. They started in ladylike fashion, by calling on the womenfolk of the triumvirs. Alas, while Octavian's sister and Antony's mother were sympathetic, Antony's formidable wife Fulvia rebuffed them. In such straits they forced their way onto the Forum, the people and the guards dividing to let them pass. They chose Hortensia, daughter of the great orator Hortensius,[1] to speak for them, and she addressed the triumvirs who, however, got angry and directed the lictors—the guards—to remove the intruders. At this, the populace began shouting. The lictors desisted and the triumvirs said they would reconsider the matter the following day. They did so and reduced both the number of women to be made to pay and the amount of their payments; the deficiency was made up by exacting a special contribution from the propertied part of the male population.

Hortensia urged that as the women had not participated in the offences of their male relations, they ought not to be penalized; that, more generally, as women were debarred from the positions of authority and the honours enjoyed by men, they ought not to be taxable; that indeed free women could not live without secure landed property; that they ought not to be taxable even in wartime; and that they certainly had no wish to finance either side in a civil war. Of the triumvirs we are told that what enraged them was not only the insolence of the challenge as such but also the women's refusal to admit that, not serving in the army like men, they should at least furnish money instead. That the women did not buy this argument is indeed refreshing: they realized that non-inclusion in the fighting citizenry was a dubious privilege.

The way the affair went off is revealing. A group of fishwives

---

[1] Both Valerius Maximus and Quintilian lay stress on the relationship. It is noteworthy that in 55 BC a speech of her father's dissuaded the consuls from a sumptuary law which they had intended: Dio Cassius 39.37.3f. According to Valerius Maximus, 'Hortensius came to life again in his female progeny', and 'if only his male descendants had been willing to emulate him, such a heritage would not have been cut off with a single address by a woman'. Hortensius's son and grandsons were indeed rather unsuccessful; see Münzer, Pauly-Wissowa, 8:2, 1913, pp. 2468f., Vonder Muehll, pp. 2478f. Valerius Maximus hints that this was their own fault: 'if they had been willing', it would have gone better. Maybe he means to convey his agreement with Tiberius's criticism: Tacitus, *Annals* 2.37f., cp. Valerius Maximus 3.5.4, 5.92f., Suetonius, Tiberius 47. Valerius Maximus's work, it will be recalled, is dedicated to Tiberius.

would have been given short shrift: they would never have reached the triumvirs. But these members of the *haute volée* were allowed to get through, helped through by humble folk, · fishermen and fishwives. When physical expulsion was ordered, once again, the bystanders and even the lictors would not go along with it. The triumvirs, seeing their attempt at firmness run into difficulties, gave way sufficiently to pacify the resisters.

Quintilian, in the last quarter of the first century AD, reports that Hortensia's speech is still read, 'and not only as a compliment to her sex'.[1] So female competition in the field of rhetoric is welcomed—up to a point. Clearly, the men feel very safe, and the note of condescension is unmistakable: there is surprise that the speech should be objectively good. Johnson was astonished to find women preaching at all,[2] Quintilian to find them do it well.

4

Let me add a few words about a woman called Beruriah who figures in the Talmud and who may be regarded as a martyress of women's civil disobedience. She lived in the middle of the second century AD, the daughter of a famous rabbi cruelly slaughtered in the Hadrianic persecution,[3] and the wife of the famous Rabbi Meir. She is the only woman in the whole of Talmudic literature to discuss points of law and theology on equal terms with the male scholars of the time. She clearly resented the prevalent contemptuous attitude displayed by the men towards the

---

[1] *Non tantum in sexus honorem.*

[2] 'Sir, a woman's preaching is like a dog's walking on his hinder legs. It is not done well, but you are surprised to find it done at all': Boswell, *Life of Johnson*, ed. Hill, rev. Powell, I, 1934, p. 463, entry of 31 July 1763. Valerius Maximus devotes chapter 8.3 to 'women whom neither natural disposition nor conventional feminine modesty succeeded in constraining to silence on the Forum and in court', *quas condicio naturae et verecundia stolae ut in foro et iudiciis tacerent cohibere non valuit.* Appian 4.5.34 describes the anger of the triumvirs at 'the women daring to assemble while the men kept quiet', *gynaikes andron hesychazonton thrasynountai te kai ekklesiasousi.* In *The Female Parliament* by Aristophanes, discussed in the first lecture, The Women of the Bible and Greece, p. 21, the heroine's name is Praxagora, 'she who acts in the assembly or in the market-place'. These and many related passages must be considered in evaluating I Corinthians 14.34: *hai gynaikes en tais ekklesiais sigatosan,* 'let your women keep silence in the churches, for it is not permitted unto them to speak'.

[3] See below, Religious Minorities, pp. 98 f.

women. Once[1] Rabbi Jose the Galilean asked her for the way: 'By which road do we go to Lydda?' 'Foolish Galilean', she replied, 'do not the Sages teach that you should not make many words with a woman? You ought to have asked, By which to Lydda?' The quotation to which she referred, the warning against much talk with a woman, is found in the *Sayings of the Fathers*.[2] Her reply to Jose's question contained two points: she was ridiculing the provincial Galilean way of speech, and she was ridiculing the rabbinical, distrustful approach to women.[3]

She was, however, made to pay dearly for her rebellious spirit. On some occasion she mocked a rabbinical adage[4] that women are light-minded, wanton. This maxim was used by the rabbis to support the recommendation[5] that a man should not be alone with two ladies to whom he is not married, though a lady may be alone with two men: the two women cannot be trusted to, so to speak, watch and guard one another while the two men can. Her husband, Rabbi Meir, warned her that she would end up by acknowledging the wisdom of the rabbinical insight. He commissioned one of his young disciples to pay court to her. After a long siege during which she remained unmoved, she started responding to him, but when she became aware of the purpose of his advances and the import of the situation, she hanged herself. Proud as she was, she could not bear the disgrace of having failed to live up to her claims. Now, however, it was Rabbi Meir who felt disgraced by her end. (In the Book of Tobit, an unhappy young woman would hang herself but for the disgrace this would bring on her father.[6]) So strong was his reaction that he changed his domicile.

The story is transmitted from an earlier source lost to us, by Rashi, the French commentator on the Talmud of the second half of the eleventh century AD. Strangely, it is misinterpreted

---

[1] Babylonian Erubin 53 b.   [2] Mishnah Aboth 1.5.

[3] An important Manuscript makes her reply: 'You ought to have asked, By which road to Lydda?' (See Goldschmidt, *Der Babylonische Talmud*, 2, 1901, p. 176.). So it is only the word *nelekh*, 'do we go', which he should have omitted. It is possible that this is indeed the word which in the original intent of the anecdote constitutes the objectionable part. It creates a link between the questioner and the lady. Substantively, to be sure, it signifies 'does one go', but formally it speaks of 'us'—a kind of *pluralis sociativus*.

[4] Preserved in Babylonian Qiddushin 80 b.

[5] Mishnah Qiddushin 4.12.

[6] Tobit 3.10. See Daube, *Novum Testamentum*, 5, 1962, pp. 99 f.

by modern historians, who make Beruriah actually succumb to her gallant. The article in the *Jewish Encyclopedia* translates Rashi's text: 'She yielded and then shame drove her to commit suicide'.[1] The correct translation is: 'She became gracious, she made herself agreeable, and when it became known to her, and when she became aware—scil. of the scheme—she hanged herself; whereupon Rabbi Meir fled because of the disgrace'. A strong argument against the prevalent view is the fact that, in Jewish tradition, Beruriah has to this day remained a revered example of a great woman. Certainly Rashi would never have told her tale if it had represented her as guilty of about the gravest sin into which a wife can fall. One might argue that the word I am rendering 'she became more agreeable', *nithrasseth*, could mean 'she yielded'. I do not maintain that this is impossible; but it would make no sense, considering the religious-cultural background, to render 'she yielded and when it became known to her' and so on: had she in fact committed adultery, the crime itself, not the exposure of her frailty, would have been the main factor in her despair. Moreover, the disciple was certainly not asked by his master to go to extremes; that would denigrate Rabbi Meir in an inconceivable degree, and nothing in the story indicates that the disciple exceeded his commission, thus incurring any reproach.

The narrative belongs to those tests of a woman's faithfulness where she is convicted before the damnable act is done. An amusing specimen of this description is Lorenzo Da Ponte's opera *Così Fan Tutte* (Mozart). In Renaissance Italy and Spain the theme of testing a woman was popular in all its variations; Shakespeare uses it in *Cymbeline*.[2] From the episode of Beruriah, as also from other materials, we may see that it goes back to antiquity. It is of course a typical product of a men-dominated world.

---

[1] Szold, art. Beruriah, *Jewish Encyclopedia*, **3**, 1902, p. 110. Henrietta Szold—a lady.

[2] In this play Imogen, after a very brief spell of going about in male disguise, concludes: 'I see a man's life is a tedious one' (Act III, Scene 6, first line). Contrast Goethe's: *Der Frauen Zustand ist beklagenswerth* (*Iphigenie auf Tauris*, Act I, Scene 1, line 24).

5

With regard both to this lecture and the one before, I ought to point out that a discussion confined to non-violent protest conveys a most incomplete picture. The advance of groups kept under by coercion commonly necessitates violent as well as civil efforts, and there is much interplay between the two. What goes on by way of bloodshed or arson greatly influences any peaceable movement, and vice versa. We like to think that violence, while playing an obviously important part in conflicts between classes, races, states, has little scope in the general development of the family once pre-history is passed. As far as the parent-child struggle is concerned, this happy belief can easily be overdone. But even in the working out of a *modus vivendi*, or *moriundi*, between the sexes, violence—admittedly never (or practically never) organized—is a not entirely negligible factor. To prove this, I need recall only a few well-known scenes.

A Biblical example is the usurpation of the royal title by Athaliah, widow of King Joram, after the death of her son, King Ahaziah.[1] In order to reign in her own right, she had all the latter's progeny, her grandchildren, killed (with the exception of one boy saved by an aunt and brought up in hiding). When we consider that her mother, Jezebel, of Phoenician provenance, had wielded enormous power as wife of King Ahab of Israel, there can be little doubt that the only female occupant of the throne of David was conscious, and proud, of her deviant role. How much of an impact it made on the general thinking about women's status we have no means of finding out; that it did make some is highly probable.

Greek literature is rich in relevant illustrations. Medea, the sorceress, was the daughter of the ruler of Colchis in Asia. It was only through her aid that the Greek prince Jason was able to steal the golden fleece from her father. With her as his wife he set out on his return voyage, and in order to delay her father who was chasing after them, she took with her her small brother, killed him, and threw his dismembered body, piece after piece, overboard; her father, collecting these bits, was slowed up. Clearly she did a great deal for her husband. Ten years the couple lived at Corinth, then Jason dismissed her in order to

---

[1] II Kings 11.1 ff., II Chronicles 22.10 ff.

marry the daughter of the king of that city. Medea sent his bride a wedding garment which burned her to death, then, before Jason's eyes, slaughtered their children, and finally flew away through the air on a chariot drawn by dragons.

All a bit extreme, but at least two general human experiences underlie the events. First, frequently a man's first wife, who selflessly helps him with his career, hails from simple conditions, or like Medea, from some less respected foreign region. Once he has reached the summit, he finds her burdensome and replaces her by a distinguished lady, suitable to his present status. Napoléon's Josephine and Marie Louise are typical. Second, the hatred of a spouse often expresses itself in making something of the children which will wound the enemy, and be it at the price of their ruin. Say, the mother is devout, precisely for this reason the father preaches atheism to the children; or the father finds the child would make a good doctor, precisely for this reason the mother steers him into the entertainment industry. The 'killing' of a child by one parent in front of the other is a common occurrence.

Medea appears on the Greek stage, the Roman, the medieval and the modern one. Two and a half millennia see in her doings and sufferings a profound reflection of the relations between husband and wife. The problems with which the legend is concerned are in constant flux. No doubt civil disobedience and indeed orderly economic, legal and moral reforms are the principal means of countering male brutality of the kind in question. Wives may be helped to retain more independence; arbitrary divorce may be made financially unattractive; its ethics may be impugned—the prophet Malachi speaks of 'dealing treacherously against the wife of one's youth'.[1] Still, it would be unrealistic to deny that violent responses—and the fear of them—have contributed their fair share to what little has been achieved.

During Agamemnon's ten years' absence at Troy, Clytemnestra took a lover, Aegisthos, and when her husband returned, helped him to assassinate the unwelcome intruder. At a certain stage of this saga she mentions as an exculpating point that, when Agamemnon was embarking on his campaign, in order to gain the favour of the gods he sacrificed Iphigeneia, their daughter. At the time Clytemnestra is arraigned, we must

---

[1] Malachi 2.14.

35

remember, it is not yet known to anyone that Iphigeneia was miraculously saved.

Originally, the saga took no account whatsoever of the feelings and rights of the mother. The enunciation of the idea that Agamemnon's action in sacrificing Iphigeneia wrongs Clytemnestra, indeed, inflicts on her so cruel a hurt that bloody vengeance becomes, if not licit, at least understandable, constitutes a momentous step towards equality.[1] Clearly, the different ways in which successive periods view her crime throw as important a light on the evolution of relations between the sexes as any incident of civil disobedience, and it makes little sense to separate off the latter.

In the present case this is all the clearer as a similar progress (surely, that is what it is) in Judaism occurs without any murderous deed intervening. In the Book of Genesis[2] God bids Abraham sacrifice his son Isaac on the Mount Moriah, and Abraham immediately sets out there, obediently, with Isaac. No thought is given to the mother, Sarah; her role is utterly irrelevant; Abraham is the master—he unhesitatingly decides to follow the command. (H. G. Wells once said he wondered whether the episode would be equally popular with parents and Sunday-school teachers if God had ordered Isaac to offer up his father Abraham and Isaac had hastened to do God's will.) In the New Testament this absolute readiness of the patriarch still receives highest praise.[3] The post-Biblical rabbis do, however, fill in the gap, at least as far as they can. They are worried about Sarah's standing and emotions; and there is a legend[4] according to which she dies from grief while the two men are away—unaware, of course, that her son will be saved by an angel's intervention at the last moment.

The story of Clytemnestra, by the way, is instructive as to a point which I shall not elaborate, but which I do want to bring to your attention. According to Homer, the actual blow that did

---

[1] See Benjamin Daube op. cit., pp. 159, 164 ff.   [2] Genesis 1.22.

[3] Hebrews 11.17 ff., James 2.31 ff. I am concerned with the neglect of Sarah. As for the sacrifice itself, the author of Hebrews considerably reduces its extreme character by making Abraham reflect on God's power to resurrect the dead: so even a slaughtered Isaac need not be lost for ever. The rabbis, too, introduce mitigations. From Genesis 22.5, 'we (plural) come again to you', for instance, they infer (Genesis Rabba 56 ad loc.) that Abraham knew Isaac would survive.

[4] Genesis Rabba 58 on Genesis 23.2.

Agamemnon in was administered by Aegisthos; Clytemnestra merely assisted.[1] In Aeschylus' *Agamemnon* she herself kills her husband.[2] Significantly, the chorus reproaches Aegisthos with baseness for leaving the execution to her.[3] The procedure described by Homer is often adopted in violent attacks on the oppressor: a male agent sympathizing with the woman does the job. Collaboration of this type, however, is of great importance also in many cases of civil disobedience. Once again, it is essential to keep in mind both areas: what goes on in one bears on the other. Antigone's fiancé, King Creon's son, at first in long debate attempts to persuade his father to revoke the death sentence. This civil protest proves futile. After Antigone's death, half insane, he rushes on his father with intent to murder him, then kills himself.[4]

Recently, Mae West was interviewed by a young lady journalist. After a while the eighty-seven-year-old artist got tired, but she was asked still to say something on the subject of women's emancipation. Barely audibly she murmured: 'I am for equal pay, equal rights.' 'Would you go on the barricades for the rights of women?' the visitor wished to know. A last time Mae West came fully awake: 'Of course, my little one, but I would have a man do it for me.'[5]

Lastly, the Danaides. The fifty daughters of Danaus escape from Libya to Argos, fleeing from the fifty sons of Aegyptus who, as their cousins, claim to have the right to marry them. Their father is hostile to the suitors and his daughters side with him. They ask the people of Argos to grant them asylum and, if need be, to defend them by force of arms against the aggressive men.

Let us pause at this point. In the eyes of some ancient bards this action constitutes (amongst other things) a protest against a custom wide-spread in antiquity: marriage imposed on a woman regardless of her wishes.[6] We shall see, when discussing slaves,[7] that the request for asylum often implied a critique of prevalent conditions. Is the disobedience non-violent? In one sense, yes: they run away. But in another sense, no: they would

---

[1] *Odyssey* 11, 409f.
[2] *Agamemnon* 1343ff. See Benjamin Daube op. cit. pp. 153ff.
[3] *Agamemnon* 1643f.   [4] *Antigone* 631ff., 1231ff.
[5] Florentine Probst in the *Stern* of 14 March 1971, p. 40.
[6] See Benjamin Daube op. cit., pp. 78ff.
[7] See below, Children and Slaves, pp. 57f.

gladly have their hosts fight a war on their behalf. In discussing Clytemnestra,[1] I pointed out this recurrent theme: the disarmed weak having their cause taken up by the well-equipped strong.

To go on, there is no war, and the sons of Aegyptus somehow manage to compel Danaus to let them wed his daughters. Danaus, however, provides the latter with weapons and orders them to kill their husbands in the wedding night. Forty-nine of them do so; one only, Hypermnestra, does not. The forty-nine who do obviously commit a deed of violence: as they have found no effective male defenders, they are driven to undertake men's work. The myth of their punishment in after-life is familiar: they must everlastingly try to fill with water a barrel which is holed—symbol of aridity. Evidently, for the authors of the myth, no appeal to the unfairness of enforced marriage can excuse such slaughter of bridegrooms.

However, Hypermnestra, who did not kill, is also brought to trial. By not killing, she offended against a daughter's duty: her father had ordered her to slay her husband. Strictly, this part of the story falls under the subject of the next lecture, Children and Slaves: the poor thing was both a woman, held down by men, and a child, held down by parents. Again, we might ask whether her disobedience is truly non-violent. At first sight it looks entirely of this kind. But one of the arguments advanced against her by her father at the trial is that the husband she has saved will murder him, so she is guilty of aiding the murder of her own father. Another argument is noteworthy:[2] by not joining her forty-nine sisters she has added to the disgrace brought upon him. If all fifty had obeyed, people upset by the massacre would not have had this special support which they can derive from even a daughter demonstrating her disapproval. This rather subtle idea pays tribute to the influence which, now and then, the criticism of the tiniest minority may exercise.

Hypermnestra is acquitted, and of the pleas on her side I mention two. First, she spared her bridegroom because he did not that night press her to do his will. This motive[3] has clearly to do with woman's aspiration to freedom and dignity. What is remarkable is that it is not a question here of enforced

[1] See above, pp. 36f.
[2] Both arguments are given by Pausanias 2 (Corinth). 19.6.
[3] Found, e.g., in Apollodorus 2.1.5.

marriage, but of the legalized rape that commonly follows upon a wedding. This one bridegroom did not perpetrate it, he respected his new wife's aversion, and that is a ground for so to speak reprieving him. I am aware that, as conceived by the ancient narrators, the defence may well have included a quibble. Danaus presumably bade his daughters perform the deed when their men were asleep after intercourse. In her case there was no 'after intercourse': so on the basis of an artificially strict interpretation, she was not bound to act. This does not alter the fact that the distinction between a husband who treats his wife as a chattel and one who treats her as a human is fully brought out.

Secondly, she spared him from love. Most versions of the saga base her disobedience to her father on this ground.[1] In modern thought love counts as a selfish motive, and a breaking of the law because of love would not count as civic resistance.[2] In the circumstances of that early period, when, generally, a daughter was rigidly subjected to her father and a wife to her husband, resistance inspired by love might be as principled and as much in the interest of society's change for the better as today, say, an appeal to equality, freedom of speech or right to work. Aphrodite who defends Hypermnestra represents her as devoted to her, the goddess, and thus as acting in the service of a worthy ideal. Towards the opening of my first lecture[3] I said that, as Helen of Troy committed adultery for pleasure's sake, she did not qualify for my inquiry into civil disobedience. Perhaps this was too narrow-minded a judgement, and we should admit that she broke a lance for a good cause. Maybe such cases should be honourably treated even today; pleasure is a value of high order.

Modern authors are greatly attracted to the forty-nine murderesses and their eternal suffering. In former periods, Hypermnestra inspired some excellent poetry. Ovid composed a letter[4] he imagined her to have written while imprisoned by her father and awaiting trial for her disregard of his command. The letter is to her bridegroom whom she had allowed to escape— the only survivor of Aegyptus' fifty sons.

---

[1] E.g. Aeschylus, *Prometheus* 865 ff., Horace, *Odes* 3.11.33 ff.

[2] Or are we in for a change? Will Gabrielle Russier—with Annie Girardot reincarnating her on the screen—live on as an Antigone in this cause?

[3] See above, The Women of the Bible and Greece, p. 1. [4] *Heroides* 14.

One way to bring into relief the interplay between civil disobedience and violence is to follow up the various causes in question, when it will become apparent that not a few sometimes evoke one kind of action and sometimes the other. Antigone and Rizpah satisfied what they considered their higher duty peacefully.[1] After Antigone had perished, however, Theseus led an Athenian army against King Creon and, being victorious, retrieved the bodies of Antigone's brother and his comrades for burial.[2] Three points to be noted. First, it was the mothers of the dead warriors who instigated Theseus to this expedition: another instance of women getting men to fight their battles.[3] Secondly, an alternative tradition insists that Theseus obtained the bodies by persuasion, without bloodshed.[4] Thirdly, Euripides, foremost exponent of the warlike version, was doubtless influenced by a recent dispute between Athenians and Boeotians, the latter being unwilling to let the former recover their fallen:[5] saga and actual life constantly influence each other.

As for burdensome taxation, the complaint of a number of ladies pounced on by the triumvirs,[6] that, in the course of history, has so frequently led to violent uprisings on top of simple refusal to pay that I may dispense with documentation.

I wish we had more information about the Amazons. There must have been a good deal of civil disobedience of men.

---

[1] See above, The Women of the Bible and Greece, pp. 5 ff., 12.
[2] Euripides, *Suppliants*.   [3] See above, pp. 36 ff.
[4] Plutarch. *Theseus* 29.4, citing Aeschylus' lost tragedy *The Eleusinians*.
[5] Thucydides 4.97 ff.; see Dieterich, s.v. Euripides, Pauly-Wissowa, **6:1**, 1907, p. 1259. By the way, I do not find Herodotus 9.27 as clearly referring to an actual battle as Dieterich thinks, p. 1258.
[6] See above, pp. 29 ff.

CHILDREN AND SLAVES

1

To set the proper background for a discussion of civil disobedience by children, a few general comments on ancient
notions of young and old are called for.[1] That old age means a
diminution of physical powers was universally recognized. That
it may adversely affect both reasoning and moral judgement was
less freely admitted; at least it is played down in the sources,
most of which come from the hands of elderly people, or at
least have passed their censorship.

There is a striking distinction between western and eastern
writings. In the former the intellectual decline of old age is
frequently and insistently noticed. There has never been a more
extreme description of the decrepitude of the old than that by
Aristotle in his *Rhetoric*.[2] In oriental writings, on the other hand,
there is greater reluctance openly to dissociate wisdom and old
age. Still, there is more evidence of that view than is generally
recognized. Throughout the wisdom tales and pronouncements
of the Bible we can detect a strand, fairly powerful, which prefers the fresh brightness of the young to the routine dullness of
the old.

Joseph, who surpasses the Egyptian professional soothsayers,
is a young man, expressly so called.[3] Solomon, at the moment
of his accession, when God bestows on him the same degree of
wisdom that Moses had enjoyed when he was eighty, is only

---

[1] I treat the problem in greater detail in my (as yet unpublished)
Edinburgh Gifford Lectures 1963, 'Law and Wisdom in the Bible',
Lecture 6, 'The Wise Judge'. Valuable observations may be found in a
book by a predecessor of mine, the Messenger Lecturer of 1967, Mme.
de Romilly: *Time in Greek Tragedy*, 1968, pp. 143 ff.

[2] 2.13.

[3] Genesis 41.12. He is only thirty at the time of his elevation by Pharaoh:
41.46.

about twenty years old.[1] In the Book of Job, the three ineffective friends are old men, but there is a fourth, Elihu, who assesses the situation far more profoundly and correctly, and who is emphatically introduced as representing young thought as opposed to old.[2] 'I am young, and you are very old, wherefore I was afraid. I said, multitude of years should teach wisdom. But great men are not always wise neither need the aged understand judgement. Behold I waited for your words, and there was none of you that convinced Job. I will answer my part, I will shew mine opinion'. The Book of Daniel is devoted to the insight and integrity of outstanding youngsters, Daniel and his comrades. His name is borne by the youthful prophet who, in the apocryphal Book of Susannah, comes to the rescue of a wrongly accused lady. Her accusers are two old men. Josephus was consulted from age fourteen on points of law by priests and officers.[3] One of the greatest early second century AD Rabbis, Ishmael, is reported to have discussed Scriptural exegesis with his teacher as an equal when even younger than that.[4] It is significant that the Dead Sea sect has a compulsory retirement age of fifty to sixty for judges and the like;[5] and in the Book of Jubilees which has affinities with that sect we are told that since the Flood, God arranged things so that man's understanding departs before his days are completed.[6] The Christian community from early on had trouble because of young people holding high office to the displeasure of their seniors: a remarkable phenomenon considering that the founder was under thirty-five when he died. The author of the First Epistle to Timothy says to his addressee: 'Let no man despise thy youth.'[7] Clearly many did do precisely that thing.

It is quite likely that in some Biblical periods there were veritable centres of young wisdom in rivalry with the more traditional ones. Such a school of young wisdom might form around the crown prince in opposition to the establishment that looked to the reigning monarch. Solomon's son and successor, Rehoboam, we are told, when facing a fundamental decision at the beginning of his reign, first consulted with 'the old men that stood before his father', and then with 'the young men (literally,

---

[1] I Kings 3.7; no reference to his youth in II Chronicles 10.6ff.
[2] 32.   [3] Life 2.9. See below, p. 49.
[4] Palestinian Aboda Zara 41 c, Song of Songs Rabba on 1.2.
[5] Zadokite Fragments 10, 14.
[6] 23.11, referred to in Zadokite Fragments 10.   [7] 4.12.

children) that were grown up with him and stood before him'.[1] In this case, the Biblical bias is against the young pretenders. But there is just too much pro-youth material to be dismissed as negligible.

I suppose in works dominated by wisdom the enthusiasm of a teacher for a magically brilliant disciple is bound here and there to break through the ordinary reverence for old age. Some instances of tribute to the young sage seem explicable in this way. Another group of writings likely to celebrate the young will be those representing a new movement or the mastery of radically new circumstances: Esther illustrates the latter though—it is important to note—she consistently acts under the guidance of her cousin Mordecai.[2]

I shall now submit some examples from the two Testaments. Remember that I shall not include violent assaults on parents, nor non-violent conduct which springs from selfish motives; say, the sons of the high priest Eli who, much to his chagrin, misused their position, defrauding the worshippers and sleeping with the female personnel.[3] To qualify for our inquiry an action must be non-violent and it must reflect some belief on the part of the child that he is right in rebelling.

One cause of disobedience to parents is a sense of national mission which is, of course, part of a more general lust for adventure, the spirit of *Jung Siegfried war ein stolzer Knab, stieg von des Vaters Burg hinab*.[4] Yet it carries a specific note. While David's three older brothers were with Saul's army, he, the youngest, had to stay behind to look after the sheep. One day, his father sent him to bring provisions to his brothers. Arrived at the camp, he heard people tell of that giant Philistine Goliath, a dire threat to the Israelites. He inquired about details, intending to do something about the mighty enemy. His eldest brother got very angry and upbraided him for his presumption: he ought to do his work at home instead of indulging in improper aspirations. David's answer is textually somewhat difficult, but it does seem to refer to an important cause which he was convinced justified his behaviour.[5]

Another area where young and old may be divided is that of

---

[1] I Kings 12.6ff., II Chronicles 10.6ff.   [2] Esther 2.10, 20, 4.13ff.
[3] I Samuel 2.12ff., 22ff.
[4] Siegfrieds Schwert, *Uhlands Gedichte und Dramen*, 1887, p. 332.
[5] I Samuel 17.12ff.; the cryptic reply is in verse 29.

possession and position. The old tend to be narrow, jealously guarding what they have; the young are inclined to be outgoing and generous. The narrative of Saul depicts the king as aware, darkly at first, more and more fully as time goes on, that David is going to succeed him and oust his house from the throne.[1] Saul's son, Jonathan, knows it too; in fact, several times he expresses this prediction.[2] Nevertheless, he contracts a profound friendship with David and sides with him against his father. This is not simply arbitrary self-will. Jonathan is attracted by David's nature and he clearly sees that this man is destined to rule: any measures Saul takes to prevent this from coming about are unjust and indeed impious. He cannot and will not manage to keep his views from his father.[3] They have words with one another, and Saul goes as far, during a particularly nasty dispute, as to throw his spear at Jonathan in order to kill him.[4] (He does the same twice to David.[5] Evidently his intent is not one hundred per cent murderous, or at least psychoanalysts would conclude this, because on all three occasions he misses.)

The narrator, although he appears chiefly to sympathize with Jonathan, does not depict Saul as a pure tyrant. The tragedy of the conflict is fully seen; there is right and wrong on both sides. In the end Saul and his son Jonathan both perish in the war against the Philistines, and David's dirge[6] pays tribute to their united death. It is one of the most moving instances of civil disobedience of a son in world literature.

Saul's daughter, whom he gives in marriage to David, deserves mention. She helps David to escape from Saul's henchmen who have been sent to kill him.[7] This may be construed as a mere act of wifely loyalty, but like Jonathan, I suppose, she feels that Saul is acting beyond his rights in attempting to eliminate David. Perhaps here too we might speak of disobedience in a high cause. She is comparable to the Hebrew midwives in Egypt rather than to Antigone for, questioned by Saul, she lies: she claims that she aided David under duress.[8] The same wife, incidentally, though so protective of David, despises his vulgar nature. As he dances in the streets on a festive occasion, clad

---

[1] I Samuel 18.8, 28, 20.31, 24.21 ff., 26.25.
[2] I Samuel 20.15, 23.17.   [3] *E.g.* I Samuel 19.4f.
[4] I Samuel 20.33.   [5] I Samuel 18.11, 19.10.   [6] II Samuel 1.17 ff.
[7] I Samuel 19.11 ff.
[8] See above, The Women of the Bible and Greece, pp. 7 ff.

44

only in a loincloth, and is applauded by the populace, her noble emotions are offended. The Bible tells us in this context that she bore him no children.[1]

If in the narrative of Saul youthful generosity is opposed to elderly rigidity and jealousy, a dramatic story in the Book of Genesis contrasts a youthful sense of honour with aged prudence.[2] The Canaanite prince Shechem seduces Jacob's daughter Dinah. Jacob hears of this while his sons, Dinah's brothers, Simon and Levi, are away. (These two are her full brothers, having the same mother as well as the same father.) He does nothing and leaves it to them to deal with the matter. No doubt he expects them to come to a peaceful if profitable understanding with Shechem's family. Shechem is eager to make full amends, to marry Dinah and indeed to submit to and join Jacob and his clan. But her brothers will have none of this. They merely pretend to accept the settlement, and then in the most treacherous fashion fall upon Shechem and his relations and slaughter them. The two brothers are fully persuaded that they should proceed as they do; and the narrator of this saga is on their side. As Jacob reproaches them bitterly for their deed, mentioning that life for him now, amidst hostile tribes, his reputation spoiled, will be terribly dangerous, they rebut him by saying: 'Should he (Shechem) be allowed to treat our sister as a whore?' They have the last word in this narrative; their sense of honour is preferred to Jacob's anxious reticence.

It is interesting that the other side, Jacob's side, nonetheless comes out in a subsequent chapter. In the final scene of the patriarch's life he extends to his sons his last wishes and forecasts. The two sons Simon and Levi are given very heavy curses: 'Cursed be their anger, fierce, and their wrath, cruel. I will divide them in Jacob and scatter them in Israel.'[3] We may conclude, then, that though whoever formulated the story of their destruction of Shechem favoured their disobedience, whoever composed the deathbed scene of Jacob condemned them for it. It would lead too far afield to enquire what different schools of thought and political-cultural conditions are behind this division.

Children may commit civil disobedience in the cause of religion. The provisions of Deuteronomy[4] impose capital punishment on a person who tries to entice you into idolatry. The

---

[1] II Samuel 6.20 ff.   [2] Genesis 34.   [3] Genesis 49.7.   [4] 13.7 ff.

people named as likely to do so are your wife, your brother, your friend, your son and your daughter, and however you love them you must not hesitate to hand them over to condign retribution. The son or daughter in this case (like the other potential seducers) is the missionary of a heathen cult, a believer, not just a self-seeker. It is interesting that your parents are not found in this list. The Deuteronomic code is addressed to the adult heads of families.[1] Hence the terrible contingency of a parent trying to make you an idolator need not be considered.

Of a rather different character is Jesus' conduct, but it too is opposed to parental direction for the sake of a deviant religious conviction. A scene recurring in all three synoptic gospels[2] is where he refuses to recognize his mother and relations because his true family, he explains, consists of those who listen to God's word. (Another relevant anecdote is contained only in Luke[3] — I shall discuss it presently.) In a sense this is an act of civil disobedience. Its original setting may have been quite specific; there are indications that his family at one stage regarded him as insane and wished to remove him from the public arena.[4]

When considering the story we must remember that people at that time were used to the fragmentation of a family into adherents to various sects. In connection with the festival of Passover, which plays such a dominant role in the New Testament, there is a particularly striking phenomenon. The original Passover meal was a family meal,[5] as it is again since the destruction of the Temple in 70 AD. But in the time of Jesus Passover was a festival of pilgrimage to Jerusalem,[6] and people who were animated by outstanding zest would go up to the capital for the occasion. Men of like mind would gather together for the journey in groups of various sizes, and the Passover Eve meal at Jerusalem would be taken by a group of pilgrims — there were countless such groups; the Hebrew word is *habhura*, 'company', 'association', 'communion'. A passover company then was a self-chosen band, *Wahlverwandtschaft*, not a biological

[1] *E.g.* 12.12, 21.18 ff.
[2] Matthew 12.46 ff., Mark 3.31 ff., Luke 8.19 ff.   [3] 2.41 ff.
[4] Mark 3.20 f. That this notice recurs in none of the other gospels is hardly surprising: it must have been a burden to popular tradition.
[5] Exodus 12.
[6] Deuteronomy 16.1 ff. For post-Biblical references, see Strack and Billerbeck, *Kommentar zum Neuen Testament aus Talmud und Midrasch*, 4, pt. 1, 1928, pp. 41 ff.

family, *Qualverwandtschaft*, and even close relations might attach themselves to different companies. Jesus, with his disciples, clearly formed one such Passover eve communion. It follows that for a son to find his true home among people of a certain colour of belief, and correspondingly to find less of a home in his natural family, would not be an unheard of thing.

We may also connect up this attitude with a general questioning in ancient philosophy as to where your true family is located. A fable by Phaedrus teaches that loving foster parents are truer parents than neglectful natural ones. It is kindness, not nature, which makes parents: *facit parentes bonitas, non necessitas.*[1]

An interesting episode is transmitted in only one of the Synoptics, in Luke.[2] Here Jesus' parents make a Passover pilgrimage with him to Jerusalem (yes, the incident is connected with Passover). He is twelve years old, that is to say, just about of age according to the Jewish custom of the time.[3] As the festival is over, his parents return homewards together with their caravan, thinking he is among the numerous troop. But they soon find him missing, search for him for a whole day and then, having discovered that he is not among the caravan, make their way back to Jerusalem. There, after a further three days of search, they find him in the Temple, engaged in theological discussion with the rabbis. This is not a minor disturbance: apart from the worry and loss of time, they will now have to journey to their home-town either without the comfort and protection of a numerous company, or with another one less familiar to them. (They had no doubt had to return to Jerusalem on their own.)

At any rate, they ask their twelve-year-old son why he has done this to them. He replies proudly: 'Did you not know that I had to concern myself about my father's (meaning my true father's, God's) business here in the Temple?' However, he then joins them and travels back home with them.

---

[1] 3.15; Perry, *Babrius and Phaedrus* (*Loeb Classical Library*), 1965, pp. 283f.

[2] 2.41 ff. Neither is there a real parallel to Luke 11.27 f.

[3] We do not know exactly when a man came of age at that time; it may have been at twelve though ultimately, thirteen was decided on. In Mishnah Niddah 5.6, a boy thirteen years old is held to his vow, one twelve years old is held to it if he understood its significance. According to R. Simeon ben Eleazar (middle of the second century AD), the ages should be twelve and eleven years: Babylonian Niddah 45 b.

The story might well have ended with the young Jesus' retort. Actually, I wonder whether at some stage it did not in fact end there. The message would have been unambiguously that the service of God, and most certainly Jesus' particular mission, takes precedence over the natural obedience tie to parents. One could conceive that at the very early period when this was the climax of the story, its aim was to give support to the usually young members of a family who, contrary to the wishes of their parents, followed the new Messianic creed.[1]

As the story stands, the retort is followed by a retreat: Jesus after all 'subjects himself' to his parents. The verb is *hypotassein*, which was technical in the rules of behaviour, the codes of community discipline, which were fashioned as the primitive Jewish-Christian sect began to crystallize.[2] It occurs, for example, in I Peter, where the younger members of the community are admonished 'to subject themselves' to the elder ones, and in the Epistle to the Hebrews where it is argued that Christians should 'subject themselves' to God as a father even worthier of reverence than an earthly one.[3] The addition of this part may well have taken place at a time when the sect was more or less consolidated, when there were a fair number of families fully Christian, that is to say, all the members being Christian. By now it was more important to stress the traditional obedience of children to parents, and of young to old, than the right and duty to break away from one's progenitors for the sake of a conviction.

My suggestion has stylistic support. The first uncompromising part is lively. Jesus is taken to Jerusalem by his parents; he at once senses his vocation and, reproved by those who would apply routine standards, silences them in the way familiar from many other encounters: 'Have you not read what David did?',[4] 'Ought not this woman whom Satan has bound be loosed?'[5]. I have labelled this tripartite form Revolutionary Action—Protest—Silencing of the Remonstrants.[6] The second conciliatory part introduces recognized, generally applicable ethics, out

---

[1] Cp. Matthew 17.29, Mark 10.29f., Luke 18.29f.
[2] On these *Haustafeln*, see Daube, *The New Testament and Rabbinic Judaism*, 1956, pp. 102ff.
[3] I Peter 5.5, Hebrews 12.9.
[4] Matthew 12.3, Mark 2.25, Luke 6.3.   [5] Luke 13.16.
[6] *The New Testament and Rabbinic Judaism*, 1956, pp. 170ff. I did not at the time include the narrative under discussion.

48

of tune with the first. That the first part is of extremely early date (not necessarily, of course, in every particular found in Luke) is indicated also by the relation of Jesus to the rabbis: his parents find him 'sitting in the midst of the doctors, both hearing them and asking them questions'. This must come from a setting where friendly though earnest controversy between believers and non-believers was still prevalent. Significantly, in the—later—Gospel of Thomas, Jesus is represented as refuting the rabbis.[1] Note also that the discourse described in Luke need not be just another specimen of a well-known genre: picturesque childhoods of heroes. From Josephus' autobiography, cited above,[2] it may be seen that (except for some details) the plot is quite realistic.

The overall effect is, at any rate, ambiguous. On the one hand there is Jesus' confident saying: he is in a higher service and they had better know it. On the other hand, the story concludes with the son following the parents. As I remarked, I think there is a development from a praise of disobedience in these circumstances to dissuasion from overmuch filial independence. But even if this is not accepted, we certainly have here a very ambivalent, barely balanced message, wavering between two duties—rebellion and submission.

Two special cases we might consider are those of the younger brother and the daughter who, disadvantaged by the law, attempt to better their status, regardless. The Book of Deuteronomy gives the first-born a double share of the estate,[3] thereby codifying a preferential treatment which, in some form or other, must have been a longstanding custom. From various narratives, however, it emerges that the younger sons were not always satisfied with this practice, and some misdeeds which are recorded may be classed as civil disobedience for the sake of legal reform. Or at least, if the deed itself was not intended to lead to reform, the narrator who preserves the memory of it may well have criticism of the prevalent injustice in mind.

The episode, where Jacob with his mother's assistance induces his blind father Isaac to pronounce the first-born's blessing over him instead of over his elder twin brother Esau, is well-known.[4] It is a civil disobedience: the tendency to

---

[1] 19.2. This Gospel (6f., 14f.) contains further colourful accounts of Jesus putting down his teachers at an even earlier age.
[2] Life 2.9; see above, p. 42. [3] 21.15ff. [4] Genesis 27.

advocate the interest of the younger over against the elder is unmistakable, especially when we remember other similar tales in the Book of Genesis, like that of Ephraim and Manasseh at the death-bed of their grandfather—who is no other than Jacob. Joseph on that occasion tries to correct his father's intention of putting the younger, Ephraim, ahead of the elder, Manasseh; but the patriarch will not be moved.[1] Let us recall that Joseph himself is a younger brother who outdistances his seniors in wisdom and success.

When we come to the daughter, Leah and Rachel are reported to have consented to an illegal enterprise in resentment against patriarchic ruthlessness.[2] Jacob, their husband, by dubious machinations, got hold of much of Laban's cattle[3] and now wished to escape, taking them with him. They agreed to follow him—in the circumstances no mean blow against Laban and, indeed, their entire family. They considered themselves in the right, however,[4] because Laban 'had sold them and quite devoured their money'. He had sold them in the sense that he had made Jacob perform long and valuable service for him in order to acquire them; and he had devoured the money in the sense that he kept all the fruits of this service himself, nothing was given to or spent on them. In their view, they had a title— by virtue of equity, one is tempted to say—to whatever Jacob had managed to seize of their father's wealth.

However self-seeking they may have been, they were breaking a lance for a general improvement in the treatment of daughters—and the public is expected to see this point of the narrative. There is no need to decide how far the regulations or conventions of the time supported Laban's meanness. These two women proclaimed the idea that a father ought not to dispose of his daughters simply in order to enrich himself and maybe the other male members of the family. If he does, his victims owe him no consideration: they may take the law into their own hands. The episode could, of course, have been discussed in my first lecture, on Women. The rebellious figures here suffered from two disabilities: that of the child and that of the female.[5]

There is a good deal of material from Greece and Rome. I

---

[1] Genesis 48.13ff.   [2] Genesis 31.1ff.

[3] See Daube, *Studies in Biblical Law*, 1947 (repr. 1969), p. 192.

[4] Genesis 31.14ff.

[5] In Numbers 27.1ff. some women submit to Moses a complaint about the laws of succession, whereupon a change is enacted. All very orderly.

shall, however, confine myself to a comedy by Aristophanes, *The Wasps*, because it is uncannily in tune with the feeling of part of modern youth.

The judicial affairs of Athens at the time were in the hands of six thousand citizens who had to be over thirty years of age, and most of them were considerably older. They were poorly paid, yet often lived on the pittance they got for attendance at sessions, so they were eager to participate in as many trials as possible. The leading statesmen made them feel very important, though in reality their power was minimal. It is not surprising in the circumstances that on the whole they were a harsh and corrupt lot. It was by five hundred and one members of this court that Socrates was tried and condemned.

Aristophanes' comedy is called *The Wasps*: the judges are brought onto the stage as hostile, stinging insects. (The coincidence with the American slang term is pretty.) The son of one of them locks up his father. He desires his father to give up his useless and cruel vocation, and to enjoy life. But the old man will have none of it. He prefers his drudgery and the consciousness that he can ruin an accused man's life to all the pleasures of the world. On the other hand, the son, simply because he is in favour of a good time for all and of not playing up to the few politicians who profit from the prevalent state of affairs, is suspected of fostering a conspiracy and of aiming to replace the democratic constitution by a tyranny. In the end he does manage to persuade his father to resign his office in exchange for the presidency of a tribunal which the son establishes for him at home. That is to say, he will be allowed to sit as judge every day from morning to night in domestic affairs. The new era is initiated by a prayer offered up by the son for the father: 'Endue him with sympathies wide, a sweet and humane disposition, which leans to the side of the wretch that is tried, and weeps at a culprit's petition.'[1] The first case tried by the father within the home is that of a dog charged with having appropriated an entire cheese, though half of it should have gone to his fellow dog. There is a distinct allusion here to the misdeeds of a prominent politician of the time. Even now, however, the father cannot give up his ingrained bitter habits, and it is only through a trick played on him by his son that his vote turns out to be 'not guilty'.

---

[1] 879ff.

That advancing age tends to make judges too stern is a theme in many cultures. Even in Talmudic law, which generally pays great deference to old age, a man who has reached the age of sixty may not sit as a judge in a capital trial—except when the crime charged is advocacy of idolatry: this is to be dealt with without mercy.[1] True, coexistent with this realization of old men's coldness is a feeling that, with their experience and discipline, they are best suited to execute justice. The highest Athenian court, the Areopagus, was composed of retired high officials, and the Ephetes, members of another important court, had to be at least half a century old.[2]

In conclusion of this discussion of children, it is my sad duty to remind you that, throughout the ages, physical assaults on parents, and the latter's fear of them, have been the strongest incentive to some relaxation on the part of those in power. At Rome, 'from as early as the second century BC, the system of absolute propertylessness of a *filiusfamilias* developed the most unpleasant creaks. Sons wished their fathers dead, and more and more frequently the wish was father to the deed. No use shutting one's eyes to it'.[3]

2

Going on to slaves—there is extremely little in the sources about civil disobedience on their part. Of violence we hear a great deal—remember Spartacus—as also of purely selfish non-violent offences—the comedy writers live by them. Of civil disobedience, very little.

This is hardly surprising. Other groups, when they resort to civil disobedience, can usually envisage success or at least ill-success short of utter disaster. A woman, for example, even in the period when the husband has absolute power over her, can hope that he will spare her out of love or out of consideration of what her family or neighbours will think; similarly, a child. By contrast it is too easy for an enraged master to do all sorts of things to a slave: beat him up, maim him, sell him, kill him. The astonishing thing is that we do come across civil disobedience at all in this field; and the few illustrations which occur are all the more interesting.

---

[1] Babylonian Sanhedrin 36 b.

[2] See Miller, s.v. Ephetai, Pauly-Wissowa, 5, 1905, p. 2825.

[3] Daube, *Roman Law*, 1969, p. 88.

There are certain exceptional situations where the risks are less extreme. For instance, a slave-woman with whom her master has fallen in love may be able to take liberties either with the master himself or with other members of the household. Pergolesi's *La Serva Padrona* has a long history. The case of Hagar in the Book of Genesis is significant.[1] (The material from the ancient Orient shows that this kind of collision was not uncommon.[2]) She belongs to Sarah who, believing herself to be incapable of bearing a child, gives her to her husband Abraham. She bears the latter a son and now becomes arrogant towards Sarah. True, she loses out; Abraham feels constrained to allow Sarah to punish her. But the narrative does show that now and then a slave might be in a relatively safe spot. Babrius[3] tells us of a slave-girl who has her master entirely at her beck and call: she can dare to quarrel with the mistress of the house to her heart's delight. Needless to add, in less rigidly heterosexual eras than ours, a slave-boy might attain the same privileged position.

One enormous difficulty in investigating civil disobedience of slaves is the dearth of literature composed by slaves. In fact, to the best of my knowledge, not a single work written by a slave while still enslaved has come down to us. We do have a number of books—not too many—by freedmen, authors who had been slaves but had gained freedom. An extremely impressive writer belonging to this class is Epictetus, who lived around AD 100, a contemporary of Plutarch and Tacitus. As Oldfather points out,[4] he uses the term 'free' with a frequency about six times that in the New Testament and twice that in Marcus Aurelius. Two other highly notable literary freedmen figures are Aesop and Phaedrus, the great fabulists.

This brings me to a more optimistic assessment. I submit that we possess considerably more direct evidence of the attitude of slaves than might at first sight appear. Perhaps the chief weapon of discontented slaves, if they did not have recourse to violence, was the word; by which I mean verbal attack on their rulers which, though it might get them into fearful trouble, yet

---

[1] 16. She is not indeed a slave in the strict sense.
[2] See e.g. Code of Hammurabi 146f.
[3] In a fable, Aphrodite and the Slave-girl: Perry, *Babrius and Phaedrus* (*Loeb Classical Library*), 1965, p. 16.
[4] Epictetus (*Loeb Classical Library*), 1, 1946, p. xvii.

they felt compelled to undertake. Phaedrus claims[1] that the fable is a genre invented by slaves who, with its help, could express thoughts and feelings which were not permitted open scope. A slave could tell a story ostensibly about animals but really referring to humans: had he told it directly about the latter, he would have incurred intolerable chastisement, whereas the roundabout criticism might just pass. It is highly unlikely that this is the truth, or the whole truth, concerning the origin of the fable. But there is no doubt that, whatever its origin, this genre was highly popular among the slave population.

There is a reason additional to that given by Phaedrus (and mind you, I take his reason very seriously: slaves did find the fable a vehicle for their grievances which they could not voice in straight language)—the level of culture among slaves. They, or many of them, were not up to the so-called higher literary forms, the polished epic, the stylized tragedy, or even the re-fined comedy. For one thing, many of these pieces were simply too long; for another, they presupposed training which slaves—most of them—had not got. The fable could reach to the lower-most stratum. It is not accidental that two of the most famous authors of fables in antiquity, Aesop and Phaedrus, had been slaves for a considerable part of their lives. Even today one need only visit the Southern region of the United States of America to understand the two factors which, combined, help a genre to take root among the oppressed: the protective shield of simile and easy access, simplicity. (The Negro Spiritual, like the fable, has both these advantages.) What I conclude is that a good many ancient fables preserve material originating or at least current among slaves.

Let me present two examples, both from Phaedrus. The first[2] is a story about an ass urged by its owner to run away together with him as hostile soldiers are approaching who would other-wise seize it. The ass asks: 'If I am captured, shall I have to carry two packs instead of one?' The owner admits: 'Well, no. One pack, just as now.' To which the beast rejoins: 'Then why should I move? It makes no difference to me for whom I carry my load as long as it remains the same.'

---

[1] 1.3, Prol. 33 ff.; Perry, *Babrius and Phaedrus* (*Loeb Classical Library*), 1965, p. 254.

[2] 1.15; Perry op. cit., p. 210.

Now in Phaedrus, this exchange is prefaced by three lines which connect it with the fate of the masses at Rome. The fable's message, according to Phaedrus, is that a change of the head of state does not affect the paupers: they simply get a new master but no really new conditions. Commentators rightly suggest that Phaedrus must have had in mind the various reversals in first-century Roman government: Seianus, the favourite of Tiberius, fell from grace in AD 31, Tiberius died in 37, his successor Caligula was assassinated in 41. But surely, except for the three initial lines, the fable sounds very much like what a slave of an independent turn of mind would hold. It is indeed a rather hefty incitement to disloyalty, to not caring a hoot. (It is that also when read in the setting provided by Phaedrus.) If it were spelled out in forthright terms, it would certainly stir up the wrath of the authorities. Just consider what happens in our time to those who openly spread this sort of advice. Why the authorities find it easier to put up with the indirect reproof I shall not here explain. (Often, alas, they will react viciously even against this.) I am not maintaining that the fable existed among slaves in the precise form it has in Phaedrus; it did not, it shows far too much his personal style. What I do suggest is that in its main outline it was handed down by slave tradition. (The Black Panthers probably do not know that Phaedrus compared himself to a panther.[1])

The other specimen[2] tells about a retort by Aesop to the ill-favoured woman who owned him.[3] He had on some occasion pointed out to her the hopelessness of her expensive efforts to attract lovers: she ought to go to bed peacefully by herself. Infuriated, she had had him flogged for this advice. Now her bracelet got stolen. She threatened her slaves with heavy blows if they failed to inform her of what they knew about the theft. Aesop, however, declared himself unmoved: 'I was beaten a

---

[1] 3.2; Perry op. cit., p. 260. He tells of a panther that fell into a pit. By a great effort in the following night she (Latin *panthera* is feminine) got out again and now the inhabitants of the district were greatly afraid of her wrath. But she announced that she would fall only on those who had clubbed and stoned her while she was helpless, not those who had been kind. Phaedrus, for a time, was in perilous disgrace with the government and probably in exile. The fable evidently dates from after his rehabilitation.

[2] No. 17 of Perotti's Appendix; Perry, op. cit., pp. 396f.

[3] I dare not recount the part she played in his release.

little while ago because I spoke the truth'. This recommendation of deceitfulness, too, sounds like having its setting among slaves. They are condemned to silence where they feel like speaking out; they retaliate by silence where the masters wish to hear them.

From Epictetus we learn that an exceptionally high-minded slave might oppose his master for the sake of philosophical truth. He writes[1] that if he were slave to a sceptic who held that the senses could never be trusted, that one could never, therefore, say what is what, he would torment him even at the risk of being victimized. When bidden by such a one to pour perfume into his bathtub, he would pour fish sauce into it and also on the idiot's head. On being reproved, he would retort that he was under the sense impression that the fish sauce was perfume and that the master's head was the bathtub. He adds that with a few like-minded fellow slaves to support the scheme, one could drive a master crazy, indeed, one could make him hang himself—or else change his silly opinion. It would be wrong to dismiss this as nothing but a day-dream or bravado, seeing that Epictetus knew well what it meant to be a slave: he was lame owing to the brutality of a master in his early years.[2]

No wonder he takes up with gusto[3] the ancient stories—true or fictitious—about Diogenes criticizing the pirates who had captured him and behaving like a master, not a slave, to the man to whom they sold him. Diogenes, it may be recalled, declared freedom of speech the most beautiful possession of a man.[4] Epictetus does admit the likelihood of flogging, chaining or other punishment if a slave conducts himself in this fashion (though fortunately Diogenes' owner recognized his superiority and freed him). This, he urges, should not deter the slave. A master who punishes his slave for expressing refined doctrines receives his own punishment by the very action he is taking against his superior. This action is contrary to human nature, so the master is doing violence to his own endowments and potentialities and suffers deterioration in consequence. By contrast the slave who is punished, or also a philosopher in a similar situation like Socrates, comes off improved. A proud programme for civilly disobedient free speech.

---

[1] *Discourses* reported by Arrian 2.20.28ff.

[2] See Oldfather, *Epictetus*, 1, 1946, p. IX.

[3] 4.1.114ff.   [4] Diogenes Laertius 6.2 (Diogenes). 69.

One type of conduct that should be considered is escape.[1] Needless to say, whenever a slave escapes, it is chiefly for selfish reasons. But in some cases an element of righteousness comes in. Certainly if the escape is so-to-speak advertised by himself, it can become almost a public protest—all the more in a period when such events happen in a somewhat concerted manner. I am thinking above all of flight to an asylum.

In antiquity, slaves who managed to reach an asylum, a temple which extended sanctuary to criminals or other persons who had to fear for their life, were often protected, at least to some degree.[2] Sometimes they became servants of the temple. Sometimes they were sold to a new master and their former master was handed the price instead of his slave. Sometimes they were handed back to their former master, but on condition that their treatment be improved—a condition he had to undertake by oath; and an oath at that time did mean some real obligation because the vengeance of the gods was feared in case of a breach. On the other hand, quite often the master succeeded in disregarding the right of asylum and retrieved his slave for terrible punishment. At any rate this flight to an asylum, or also, say, to the statue of a god, a king or an emperor which had to be respected, was a more or less public act which' especially in a period when such incidents occurred with frequency, might assume the character of a more than selfish challenge: something in the nature of civil disobedience. We may note that, as in other types of civil disobedience on the part of slaves, the situation was such that the slave had a chance' however slight, of a measure of success.

In particular in Imperial Rome, gradually the law recognized this procedure, i.e., tamed it, and with a good many reservations gave it a legal standing. In other words, rules were evolved laying down that, given certain conditions, a slave who had taken himself to a designated place would be heard and given some relief. It is significant that, in early classical law, in the first century AD, a slave who has fled to the Prefect of Rome was treated as a fugitive in the technical sense, which meant degradation, whereas by the end of the second century he no longer

---

[1] For Imperial Rome, there is a recent investigation: Bellen, *Studien zur Sklavenflucht im römischen Kaiserreich*, 1971. I dealt with a certain aspect in *Juridical Review*, **64**, 1952, pp. 12 ff.
[2] Cp. Deuteronomy 23.16 and Paul's Epistle to Philemon.

counted as a fugitive.[1] This kind of civil disobedience has by now become a recognized institution. It is no longer disobedience.

A full treatment of this subject might also take account of the Saturnalia, a festival where—within limits—the master became slave and the slave became master. On this one occasion a slave's feeling that there was no inherent justice in his lowly status could be expressed without breaching law and convention.

It would give the wrong picture if I omitted mention of a very different type of civil disobedience by children and slaves, namely, illegal support of a father or master. One form of it is the commission of a crime at his behest or participation in his criminal activity. Roman law made some allowances for a son's or slave's bind, when he was caught between fear of, or loyalty to, his immediate superior and the criminal ordinances of the state. For example, a man contracting a bigamous marriage suffers no infamy if he was ordered to do so by his head of family.[2]

Another variant is striking: we know of sons and slaves who, when the father or master was hunted by the party in power or charged with a serious crime, even under torture refused to betray him.[3] Cicero's brother, when proscribed by the triumvirs Augustus, Antony and Lepidus in 43 BC, was concealed by his son and the latter withstood the grimmest tortures. However, the father could not let it go on and gave himself up: both were put to death.[4] In the year 65 AD a conspiracy against the hateful emperor Nero was discovered and it was essential for that tyrant to get to know as many details as possible. Among those arrested was a freed woman—not any longer a slave, but having been a slave and having acquired her freedom. She was one of the very few who never under the severest torture gave away anything, and when hardly able to move a limb, managed to commit suicide. Tacitus' eulogy of her is noteworthy:[5] 'An emancipated slave and woman, by shielding under this dire coercion men unconnected to her and all but unknown to her,

<hr>

[1] See Bellen op. cit., p. 74.
[2] Digest 3.2.1; see Daube, *The Defence of Superior Orders in Roman Law*, 1956, p. 17 (also published in *Law Quarterly Rev.*, **72**, 1956, p. 508).
[3] For the Republic, see Kroll, *Kultur de Ciceronischen Zeit*, **2**, 1933, p. 87.
[4] Dio 47.10.7.   [5] *Annals* 15.57.

she had set an example which shone the brighter at a time when persons freeborn and male, Roman knights and senators, untouched by the torture, were betraying each his nearest and his dearest.' Quite a few similar cases involving slaves proper (not freedmen) are recorded in the sources.

What induced children or slaves to incur mutilation and death for the sake of a father or master I shall not here inquire. Between parents and children there may, of course, be a positive, warm relationship; and in an era when, as a rule, the treatment of a slave is at best distant, at worst, terrible, an outstanding master's kindness may go a long way to evoke fervent gratitude.

Unfortunately, it is not safe to infer, whenever a subordinate saves his superior at high cost to himself, that this must be in response to decency and humanity. The younger Seneca's advice[1] that a slave allowed to talk to his master will be reliable and vice versa is sound so long as we are alive to the numerous exceptions. Dogs may be deeply attached to cruel masters and the same happens in the human world. It happens in the case of both slaves and children, not to forget women—the most faithful wife does not necessarily belong to the kindliest husband. In the same troubles in which the Ciceros perished, a slave who had been branded by his master for attempting to escape rescued the latter at fearful risk.[2] But I shall not pursue this aspect of my topic. I ought perhaps to remark that what constitutes decency and what cruelty is not so easy to judge.

Nor shall I go into the question in what circles and in what kind of literature the memory of faithful slaves is cultivated. Valerius Maximus, for example, has a chapter 'On the Loyalty of Slaves'.[3] The immediate, general answer is obvious: we know who has the chief interest in a self-sacrificing attitude of the downtrodden. Yet once we probe the matter in depth, it turns out to be quite complicated. I shall leave it at that.

---

[1] *Epistles* 47.4.   [2] Dio 47.10.4f.   [3] 6.8.

PROPHETS AND PHILOSOPHERS

1

Before I enter into a discussion of prophets and philosophers I would advert to what are probably the earliest heroes of civil disobedience.[1] In the case of prophets and philosophers, as in fact of all civil disobedience in the ordinary sense, the deviant offends some earthly power structure. In very ancient thought there is a stage prior, almost, to any divisions in society where man strives with a hostile god or a number of hostile gods. Man, persuaded of his right or even duty to forge ahead, has to confront a god jealous of human progress.

In the Greek myth, as Zeus, the highest of the gods, is intent on withholding from man the basic material for civilization, namely fire, Prometheus, a being half-way between the Olympian rulers and the earth-dwellers, steals the forbidden object from heaven and brings it to man. Zeus cannot undo what has been done; he can only inflict dire punishment on the two conspirators, Prometheus and man. The myth reflects an archaic phase in theology when man looks on the gods as opposed to him. Nor can one be surprised that there should have been such a phase seeing that, before the advent of even primitive technology, it must have been very natural for man to feel himself in the midst of a largely inimical set-up. Any gains were to be attained in defiance of the dominant forces around him.

---

[1] They are discussed in my (unpublished) Edinburgh Gifford Lectures 'Law and Wisdom in the Bible', 1963, in the Lecture 'Justice in the Narratives'. For a survey of parallels to Genesis 2.15 ff., see Graves and Patai, *Hebrew Myths, The Book of Genesis*, 1964, pp. 76 ff.; and for a comparison of the Tower of Babel with allied Greek legends, see my brother Benjamin Daube's remarks, *Zu den Rechtsproblemen in Aischylos' Agamemnon*, 1938, pp. 130 ff. On the *Streitgespräche* like Abraham's intercession for Sodom, I have commented in *Von Ugarit Nach Qumran* (Festschrift Eissfeldt), 1958, pp. 38 ff.

In the Bible, one of the chapters representing this stage is the so-called story of the Fall.[1] It ought to be entitled the story of the Rise. It is only if we read it through late Jewish rabbinical and Christian spectacles that it is about a fall. It is indeed astonishing that the true meaning should have been success-fully suppressed so long, undiscovered even by the majority of modern critical investigators. Stripped of subsequent interpre-tation, the narrative reports that Adam and Eve were in a garden, living crudely and mindlessly like the animals sur-rounding them. 'They were naked and not ashamed'—this, from the wisdom narrator's point of view, was not a blissful, Rousseauesque state but a horrible primitivity.[2] However, there was a tree in the garden with knowledge-giving fruit. Only God forbade the couple to eat of it, and he made sure his pro-hibition would be heeded by threatening them with immediate death if they disobeyed: 'On the day that you eat thereof, you shall assuredly die.'[3] A being half-way between God and man, the serpent, informs them that the threat is empty: the fruit is not death-bringing, not fatal, on the contrary it will open their eyes and make them discerning. So they do eat of it, and indeed God turns out to have been lying. They do not die, and their eyes are opened exactly as the serpent, the Prometheus of the Biblical story, told them. They become discriminating between good and evil, aware of their nakedness—capable of shame. Just like Zeus, God inflicts fearful retribution on the rebellious serpent and couple, but like Zeus, he must put up with the start of human civilization.

Another anecdote from that phase of theology is that of the Tower of Babel.[4] The inhabitants of the earth want to build a city where they can all live together. This would be an ideal world. For those who forged this myth, the city represents culture, a living together in a worthy manner; and such an all-embracing foundation would insure continued progress and peace. But the jealous God destroys the enterprise and dis-perses those who have attempted it: thus is created permanent

---

[1] Genesis 2.15 ff.
[2] Genesis 2.15. In Deuteronomy 25.11 the male genitals are called *mebhushim*, 'the shameful parts', 'the parts to be ashamed of' (see Daube, *Orita*, 3, 1969, p. 37). By the time of Zephaniah 3.5, it is the obtuse scorner of justice—not the obtuse savage—who 'knows no shame'.
[3] Genesis 2.17.   [4] Genesis 11.1 ff.

division into different languages with its corollary of permanent disunion.

In both narratives, that of man's Rise and that of the Tower of Babel, according to the author's intent, man acts from a belief in his destiny and improvement. It is remarkable that in the former story man succeeds at the price of being punished; in the latter he does not succeed. After all, basic culture, the fire in the Greek myth, the power of discrimination in the Hebrew one, did come about, whereas a united mankind, everyone understanding everyone else, has not been achieved to this day.

Presumably, though these tales pit man against God, they are to some extent modelled on precedents involving struggles of man against man. They indicate acquaintance with a milieu where a potentate can only with difficulty be got to concede a minimum of independent life to his subjects. They also suggest attempts by the latter to win more freedom, be it by getting hold of resources previously controlled by him alone, be it by overcoming disunion and congregating. There may be a reminiscence, too, of a helpful role of persons who, while connected with the ruler, side with the oppressed—and pay the price.

In somewhat later stories, though there is still a degree of divine reluctance to tolerate or initiate human progress, the disobedience has been weakened into argumentation with God; as when Abraham disputes God's right to destroy the entire city of Sodom should there be even a small band of righteous men living there[1] (Moses and Aaron have to reiterate this restriction on divine retribution[2]), or as when the king of Gerar disputes God's right to put to death a man who has committed adultery, not knowing that the woman in question was married to someone else.[3] These narratives (of which the Book of Job is, in a sense, an offshoot) no longer fall within the purview of our theme.

2

I proceed to the prophets, and let us agree to define them as direct transmitters and performers of God's will. To go by the Biblical account, up to the advent of Saul, the Hebrews were ruled by them. Abraham is expressly called by this term;[4]

---

[1] Genesis 18.20ff.   [2] Numbers 16.22.
[3] Genesis 20.1ff. On some aspects of the case see my *Sin, Ignorance and Forgiveness in the Bible*, 1960, pp. 7ff.   [4] Genesis 20.7.

Jacob's forecasts on his death-bed are familiar;[1] Joseph ex-
pounded dreams;[2] Moses has remained the ideal prophet to
this day,[3] and his disciple Joshua and the so-called Judges
followed in his footsteps;[4] Deborah, a prophetess, was one of
them.[5] Throughout that long epoch, then, there was no cleavage
between government and prophets; the government was in the
latter's hands. Accordingly, there was no room for disobedience, civil or violent, on their part. Indeed, as far as violence
is concerned, they waged war against external enemies and
punished, decimated and got rid of their enemies within, like
any other government.

My picture is admittedly a bit simplified. One extraordinary
episode[6] deserves notice because of its after-effects: Phinehas,
a grandson of Aaron's, when Moses seemed passive in the face
of the men beginning to introduce heathen women into the
camp, speared one of the detestable couples. This was a spon-
taneous outburst of religious fury, ratified, however, by God
who informed Moses of his full approval. The incident occupied an important place in post-Biblical Judaism, as showing
that there comes a moment when extreme supra-legal action is
called for. He counted as the first zealot.[7]

About 1000 BC the people asked the last such prophet-ruler,
Samuel, to institute a kingship on the Canaanite model.[8] He
took it very amiss and so, indeed, did God: the petitioners preferred henceforth not to be led by God's immediate messengers.
Yet, though the request meant a rejection of the perfect order,
it was acceded to and Samuel, at God's bidding, anointed
Saul. The case furnished Jewish jurisprudence with an exemplar
for institutions the law recognizes by way of concession to
human frailty: thus, for Jesus, divorce was admitted by Moses
'for the hardness of your hearts'.[9]

So now there was a dichotomy between the head of the state
and God's representatives. Moreover, the prophets, since they
had been in actual charge, were not, as in other cultures, just expert in higher requirements. Antagonism between the pursuers

---

[1] Genesis 49.1ff.   [2] Genesis 40.5ff., 41.1ff.   [3] Deuteronomy 34.10.
[4] Joshua 1, Judges 2.6ff.   [5] Judges 4.4.   [6] Numbers 25.
[7] I Maccabees 2.26, 54, Jerusalemite Targum on Exodus 6.18, Babylonian Sanhedrin 82 af., Sota 22 b.
[8] I Samuel 8f. See Daube, *J. of Jewish Stud.*, **10**, 1959, pp. 1ff., and
California Law Rev., **59**, 1971, pp. 787ff.
[9] Matthew 19.8, Mark 10.5.

of secular interests and the advocates of the deity's intentions is indeed universal: it exists, say, between Pharaoh and his soothsayers [1] or Moses. [2] But within the Hebrew state, as the prophets started out as inheritors of the true leaders, it assumed a particular form. For a while, up to a point, they went on being treated as the decisive voice in the direction of the community; and as a result, in the reports about their confrontations with various kings, it is frequently the latter who are depicted as deviant, disobedient. The first king, Saul, was expected to be utterly subservient to Samuel, being reproved for any sign of autonomy; [3] and both in his case and that of David there were moves to make them into prophets themselves, so as to bridge the gulf. [4] Strictly, from the point of view of the desert tradition, the tradition harking back to the era when rulership lay with the direct agents of God, the entire institution of the monarchy constituted an act of tolerated civil disobedience.

It is chiefly this development which explains the prophets' employment of combatant or non-combatant means. For a considerable period under the kings, we have seen, they maintained much concrete power. During that era, they were far from averse to violence. Samuel with his own hands killed the Amalekite king whom Saul had spared. [5] Elijah resorted to extraordinary brutality: on one occasion he had all the priests of the sanctuaries serving Baal, the false god, captured, and himself slaughtered them—hundreds of them—to the last man. [6] It is only in the course of time that civil conduct came to prevail among the prophets. As so often, the turn from force towards persuasion was due not only to a change in moral judgement, but also to a decrease in material resources: violence was no longer feasible.

Where the prophet opposes the authorities non-violently, his weapon will be the word alone, addressed sometimes privately to the king, sometimes to the public at large. To some extent this distinction coincides with another: a dissenting prophet may wish ultimately to help the government by his rebuke, to put it on the right path so that it be safe, or he may be out to bring it down because it is utterly wicked. In the former case, as a rule, private reprimand will be preferred; in the

---

[1] Exodus 8.15, 9.11.   [2] Exodus 5 ff.   [3] I Samuel 10.8, 13.8 ff.
[4] I Samuel 10.6, 10 ff., 19, 20 ff., II Samuel 6.14 ff.
[5] I Samuel 15.9 ff.   [6] I Kings 18.40.

latter, public condemnation. When Nathan upbraids David for his misdeeds, and even when he announces severe punishment, he is nevertheless desirous of thereby securing David's and his house's reign.[1] Similarly, when Shemaiah declares against the punitive expedition King Rehoboam plans, he does so because the war would be disastrous, and though the king may resent interference, he is in fact saved by it.[2] On the other hand, there are the public charges Elijah levels against Ahab.[3] Samuel, while Saul is king, anoints David, thereby making an end to the house of Saul: he does not confine himself to a private debate with the latter. Significantly, at a time when the king, though already at loggerheads with Samuel, is still to exercise his office, the prophet consents to pay him homage in public.[4] Elisha, during Ahab's reign, anoints Jehu and, indeed, instructs him to wipe out the reigning family[5]—so this is hardly just civil disobedience. There are all sorts of gradations, just as today civil disobedience may be basically in support of the system—some of the religious sects provide examples—or it may aim at its destruction, or it may lie anywhere in between.

Just as today, the prophet's conduct may often amount to treason, or near-treason, be it that it is designed to overthrow or gravely upset the regime from within, be it that it favours a foreign enemy. The anointment of a pretender by Samuel and Elisha clearly constitutes treason of the former kind. Shemaiah's opposition to Rehoboam's war project, if a hostile interpretation were put upon it, might be said to be less than patriotic. It is well known that the major prophets were often extreme obstructionists in regard to the government's external involvements. I shall make some comments on Jeremiah below.[6]

Whether ultimately a friend of the powers-that-be or a foe, the prophet is more profoundly conscious than anyone else of a mission imposed on him. Others may feel called on to resist from conscientious scruples; none bears the same inescapable burden as the prophet who, after all, speaks on behalf of God. He has to go through with his task, come to him what may.

One of the most famous stories in the Pentateuch,[7] a very early one, that of Balaam's ass, though it refers to a heathen

---

[1] II Samuel 12.1ff.
[2] I Kings 12.22ff., II Chronicles 11.2ff. See below, Aspirants to Statehood, p. 129.
[3] I Kings 18.17ff. [4] I Samuel 15.30f., 16.1ff. [5] II Kings 9.1ff.
[6] See pp. 67ff. [7] Numbers 22.21ff.

prophet, is intended to illumine this role. More precisely, it is meant to show how a prophet faithfully serving his government must resist the latter and suffer in order to save it. It is remarkable that the significance of this familiar chapter has so far eluded its commentators.

Balaam, you may remember, a heathen seer, is hired by Balak, the heathen king of Moab, to curse the Israelites as a preliminary to a successful war. They are on their way through the desert under the leadership of Moses, and Balak wishes to fall upon them. Balaam however, in deference to God's command, utters a blessing, thus making it impossible for Balak to execute his designs. Balak is infuriated. Nevertheless, he does give up his proposed attack, and is thereby rescued—rescued against his evil will: he continues in his peaceful reign over Moab.[1]

Now what about the ass? The ass, by an analogous act of civil disobedience, saves Balaam as he is on his way to meet Balak. An angel, not noticed by him, repeatedly bars the road with a sword in his hand, ready to slay him. The ass sees more than the master. It does notice the angel and each time he threatens Balaam it refuses to proceed, even though Balaam resorts to cruel beating. The ass complains: 'Have I not always been of help to you, and carried you loyally, yet you punish me.' But Balaam cannot at this moment appreciate the sense of the animal's obstreperousness. In the end the angel reveals himself to him and he has to admit that he owes his life to his disobedient, faithful beast.

In a way, the story may be compared to the much later Book of Jonah, distinguished by a marvellous working-together of God, man, animals and inanimate nature. At any rate, the ass follows a higher duty, contrary to the immediate orders of its master. The latter, Balaam, is going shortly to do the same, and his disobedience also proves to be the salvation of the person whom ostensibly it offends. The ass's conduct pre-enacts Balaam's—even in details: it is refractory three times, just as

---

[1] The first half of Joshua 24.9 should be rendered, not 'Then Balak . . . arose and warred against Israel', but 'Then Balak . . . arose and he was going to war against Israel'. The second half of verse 9 and verse 10 tell us how God vitiated his plan by making Balaam bless the people he intended to attack. The meaning of 24.9, first half, that is, is not that it actually came to a war. It refers only to the Moabite king's intention—in perfect accordance with the narrative in Numbers.

Balak asks Balaam three times to curse Israel and each time the seer conscientiously utters a blessing instead.[1]

One reason the message of this fable in regard to the seer's civil disobedience has not been seen is surely that the Bible, as one would expect, places emphasis on the escape of the Israelites effected through Balaam's oracle: that oracle showed them to be favourites of God, not to be assaulted, and Balak listened to it. But the other consequence is equally unmistakable: namely that Balak, too, is kept free from harm. However unwillingly, he returns home in compliance with Balaam's God-dictated utterances. The fable may indeed be of Moabite provenance, primarily celebrating Balaam's faithful fulfilment of a heavy task, and the resulting good that came to the Moabite king. It should be observed that, in a number of passages, Balaam is represented as no less hostile to the Israelites than is Balak.[2] In order to prevent the latter from a disastrous enterprise, he must bless them, but he does so *contre coeur*:[3] he remains impenitently in the opposite camp, looks on them as hateful intruders. Again, the speaking animal is such an exceptional character in the Pentateuch that alien origin is not at all unlikely. If that were so, then there was a far stronger Canaanite influence even on the higher spheres of Hebrew prophecy than we are generally inclined to assume: the Hebrews would at a very early stage have encountered a mature, sophisticated model of one phase at least of the prophet-king relation.

One more point: at the beginning of my first lecture,[4] I stated that, contrary to the more orthodox current approach, I do not hold that a person, to qualify as civilly disobedient, must be prepared to undergo the legal consequences. It is noteworthy that Balaam's ass, and its master also, do take the consequences of their conscientious obstinacy. The ass is flogged, Balaam—for whom the animal sets the example—is dismissed by the king in great anger. So here you have your earliest precedent for this readiness to accept the penalty, long before Socrates—an ass!

Let me leap across several centuries. In the year 587 BC the prophet Jeremiah was thrown into a dungeon to be kept in strict custody.[5] A Babylonian army was besieging Jerusalem

---

[1] Numbers 22.28, 33, 24.10.   [2] Numbers 31.8, 16, Joshua 13.22.
[3] Very clear in Deuteronomy 23.6.
[4] See above, The Women of the Bible and Greece, pp. 3f.
[5] Jeremiah 37.11ff.

and he predicted defeat to his compatriots. He counselled surrender in order to avoid worse: destruction of the city and deportation of its inhabitants. But the king put his trust in Egyptian promises of help and continued resistance.[1] Jeremiah was arrested as he was leaving Jerusalem by a gate. It was generally thought that he was about to desert: understandable, seeing that he openly exhorted the populace to run away to the enemy.[2] He denied the charge; perhaps maintaining[3] that, on the contrary, he had only intended to visit a field which belonged to his family, and which, indeed, he was preserving as family property at considerable cost in order to indicate that the Babylonians would not forever be masters of the country, and that Jewish ownership would in the end prevail.[4] However, as I remarked, he was imprisoned. Yet the king entertained secret communication with him, desirous to know his views, however unwelcome they sounded.[5] In the end the Babylonians did that year take the city, and while the king and an enormous number of citizens were deported, Jeremiah received honourable treatment at the hands of the conquerors.[6]

Some three hundred years later, in the first half of the third century BC, there was at the court of King Ptolemy Philadelphus of Egypt a writer of tragedies, by name of Lycophron. He wrote a long piece about Cassandra, the daughter of King Priam of Troy, who had foreseen the fall of her city and family, but whose prophecies had not been believed. Lycophron introduces into her life a feature we do not find in any earlier literature about her: she is kept imprisoned with a guard to prevent her escape, and also to keep anyone unauthorized from communicating with her. King Priam however, wants to know her views, and the guard has to give him a precise report of her raving utterances.

It has been suggested[7] that this innovation of Lycophron's,

---

[1] Jeremiah 34.1ff 1, 37.3ff.   [2] Jeremiah 21.9, 38.2.
[3] This is suggested by Jeremiah 37.12, if we translate 'he went forth out of Jerusalem into the land of Benjamin, to fix there his share in the midst of the people' (i.e. among his kin). However, the final clause may mean: 'to escape from there (i.e. Jerusalem) in the midst of the people (i.e. with the many other fugitives)'; see Westbrook, *Israel Law Rev.*, **6**, 1971, p. 368.
[4] Jeremiah 32.   [5] Jeremiah 37.17ff., 38.14ff.
[6] Jeremiah 39.11ff., 40.1ff.
[7] See Bethe, art. Kassandra in Pauly-Wissowa's *Real-Encyclopädie*, **10**: 2(20), 1919, pp. 2291f. Ziegler, art. Lykophron, in **13**: 2 (26), 1927,

Cassandra's imprisonment, has a merely technical purpose: it is a device to introduce a person, namely the guard, who, being constantly around, can set out her prophecies in all detail. There may well be something in this proposition, but it seems to me a far from full explanation, considering the striking parallel of Jeremiah. I do not for a moment suggest that Lycophron drew on the Biblical precedent (despite the interest in the Old Testament attributed to Ptolemy Philadelphus). The similarity is due to a trait inherent in the situation—a trait characterizing the prophet of doom. On the one hand, it will always be tempting for a government to put him away; he creates doubt and disaffection, he undermines what morale there is.[1] One may be afraid to destroy him, but he had better be locked up. It is interesting that in Homer's Troy, Cassandra was left free: clearly, the Ptolemaic monarchy is less tolerant, so Lycophron places her in custody.[2] On the other hand, the leader of the movement or the country or the family against whom the prophet's threats are directed may have an irrepressible urge to learn his opinions. This is how we have to explain the coincidence, Jeremiah incarcerated and questioned by the Jewish king, Lycophron's Cassandra, incarcerated and questioned by King Priam.

There is a very early Old Testament precedent: Saul's tragic inquiry from the witch of Endor on the day before his last battle.[3] Moreover, some fifteen years before his arrest, Jeremiah himself had a not dissimilar experience with an even more wicked king.[4] On that occasion the king was informed of a prophecy of ruin which Jeremiah's disciple, Baruch, had written down at his master's dictate. The prophecy had been publicized among the populace and had created a tremendous impression unfavourable to the king's policy. The king asked that the roll be fetched and read out to him. As it was being recited he cut off each little section and threw the work piece-

---

thinks that already the Cyclic poets or Bacchylides may have represented her as shut up, but he makes no guess about their motivation. Quintus Smyrnaeus 12.525 ff., incidentally, often supposed to draw on the Cycle, knows nothing of her imprisonment.
[1] Jeremiah 38.4: 'Let this man be put to death, for thus he weakens the hands of the men of war that remain in this city and the hands of all the people.'
[2] Or if the idea goes back to Lycophron's source, then the regime envisaged by that source is less tolerant than the Trojan.
[3] I Samuel 28.3 ff.   [4] Jeremiah 36.1 ff.

meal into the fire. So he burned the whole of it, but, significantly, not without having taken it in. This drama, incidentally, took place about two hundred years before the burning
of a treatise by Protagoras and four hundred years before the
burning of the books in China, to which two events I shall
briefly advert below.[1]

A remark on Jeremiah's conduct at that time. The king who
destroyed the roll would have liked to eliminate the author, but
Jeremiah went into hiding. This flight has been unfavourably
contrasted with Elijah's fearless confrontation with his
monarch,[2] also with John the Baptist's challenge of King
Herod.[3] Such comparisons take no account of what a prophet
wants to achieve. Jeremiah many a time proved his unlimited
personal courage. Even Elijah, when he felt the moment for
direct collision had not come, looked for security.[4] John the
Baptist did not run after the first opportunity—there must
have been many—of having it out with the authorities, and
Jesus fled when that seemed the right thing for his task.[5] It is
not the job of a prophet, or indeed any fighter for a cause, to
satisfy the unhealthy fantasies of inexperienced theorists. The
midwives in Egypt, we saw in the first lecture, by duping
Pharaoh, succeeded in carrying on their fruitful work.[6]

It used to be widely held[7] that true and false prophets can be
distinguished by the former foretelling woe, the latter, good
fortune. This is a gross simplification. What is true, however,
is that there is a close connection between the prophet of doom
and civil disobedience. The prophet of good fortune is welcome
to the party in power. It is the prophet of doom who violates
the dominant interests, and is apt to go beyond what the rulers
can safely tolerate; he is also apt to refrain from violence, be it
on the ground of morality, be it on that of material weakness.

When we consider the extreme contempt and hostility shown
by many ancient seers and prophets to the authorities, and
often in critical situations, when the latter were involved in a

---

[1] See p. 72.   [2] I Kings 21.17 ff.
[3] Matthew 14.4, Mark 6.18, Luke 3.19.   [4] I Kings 19.3 ff.
[5] Matthew 12.15 f., 15.21, Mark 1.45, 3.7, 7.24, John 8.59, 10.39 f.
[6] See above, The Women of the Bible and Greece, p. 9. A sound
treatment of Jeremiah's attitude is found in Rudolph, *Jeremia*, 3rd ed.,
1968, p. 235.
[7] Partly on the basis of passages like Jeremiah 28.8 f. Rudolph op. cit.,
pp. 179 ff., gives a balanced interpretation.

life-and-death struggle, the amazing thing is not that the prophet of doom sometimes suffered, but that he so frequently got away with it. A protective device—one of a number—was riddling language. Plutarch, in his treatise on the Delphic oracle,[1] claims that a major reason that oracle spoke in the well-known ambiguous manner was that a powerful questioner should not be provoked if the reply was not to his liking. The Hebrew prophets also, on many occasions, clothed their unfavourable forecasts in language not immediately obvious to the uninitiated. And of course, the veil of allusion serves as a precaution against overwhelming, ill-intentioned authority in the New Testament no less than in the Old. We need only remember the 'abomination of desolation' quoted from Daniel in the Gospels of Matthew and Mark, with the addition 'let him who readeth understand'.[2] In my previous lecture[3] I mentioned a genre popular among slaves, the fable, and its advantage as to some extent disguising ideas which, if expressed openly, would lead to victimization. During the Second World War, Jean-Paul Sartre had a play performed which the occupying Nazis apparently did not see for what it was, so cleverly was the Resistance character glossed over. Yet the French audiences did understand. Future historians of our time will find it a fascinating study to discover the various degrees of veneer authors use in order to pass, and not to be persecuted, or even prosecuted,[4] for dangerous views. Your present lecturer is something of an adept at—to use a phrase of Heraclitus[5]—neither telling nor concealing but indicating. To speak through historical figures is sometimes wiser than to declare in one's own name. The word 'person' originally means a mask, something to 'persound', to sound through.[6] Civil disobedience can at all times profitably avail itself of persons.

---

[1] 25.407 Cff. Other elements contributing to the ambiguous style of oracles are listed by Parke and Wormell, *The Delphic Oracle*, 2, 1956, pp. XXIIIf.
[2] Matthew 24.15, Mark 13.14, Daniel 9.27, 11.31, 12.11; see Daube, *The New Testament and Rabbinic Judaism*, 1956, pp. 418ff.
[3] Children and Slaves, pp. 54ff.
[4] Maybe the latter is less horrid than the former?
[5] Quoted by Plutarch 21.404 Df.; Diels, *Die Fragmente der Vorsokratiker*, 7th ed. by Kranz, I, 1954, p. 172.
[6] If we believe Bassus: Gellius, *Attic Nights* 5.7. The root may, however, be Etruscan.

Socrates was not the first thinker tried for *aseby*, impiety. (That was in 399 BC.) Several men had preceded him, Aeschylus (accused around 460 BC), Anaxagoras (450 BC) Andocides (415 BC), Diagoras (411 BC) and Protagoras (411 BC), as well as a lady, Pericles' mistress Aspasia (around 434 BC). Aeschylus was acquitted; Aspasia narrowly escaped being sentenced; the other four had to go into exile, and Anaxagoras may have committed suicide. Later figures charged or nearly charged are Stilpon, Euripides and Aristotle.

Protagoras, by the way, had published a book opening with the statement that he did not know whether the gods did or did not exist. The authorities sent a herald through Athens to collect all copies and had them burned in the market-place[1]—the first burning of this kind I have come across. King Jehoiakim, we saw,[2] in 604 BC threw a hostile prophecy of Jeremiah's into the fire at which he was sitting while it was read out to him: that was not, primarily, an act of censorship, it was meant as a demonstration of utter contempt for the message. Far more comparable is the burning of all philosophical treatises—among them Confucius's Analects—condemned by the Legalists in China in 213 BC. It was designed to put an end to 'the hundred schools of thought'. (Mao's dictum[3] encouraging 'a hundred flowers to blossom, a hundred schools to contend' alludes to and repudiates that repressive measure.) In the same year, as it happens, the Roman government burned a large number of books with—from its point of view—dubious oracular forecasts which, at the height of the second Punic war, enjoyed a dangerous popularity.[4] Tacitus, after reporting that Nero ordered the burning of certain books attacking senate and priesthood, adds: 'They were eagerly sought after and read so long as they were to be procured at a risk; freedom to have them in no time led to oblivion.'[5]

So much has been written on the subject of Socrates' death that I shall draw attention only to a few particularly relevant items. To begin with, for the harshness of the verdict. Four

---

[1] Diogenes Laertius 9.52.   [2] See above, p. 70.
[3] In his speech of February 27, 1957, 'On the correct handling of contradictions among the people'.
[4] Livy 25.1.12; cp. Livy 39.16.8.   [5] Tacitus, *Annals* 14.50.

points are here worth mentioning. First, he himself compared his conduct to that of a gadfly that fastens on a horse and will not let it slumber.[1] He constantly questioned young and old as to their reasons for the way they lived their lives, and in doing so satirized deep-rooted values and habits. In any society, and especially in one finding itself beleaguered on all sides by deadly enemies, this is upsetting, worrying, and is felt to be anything but innocuous: it threatens what remains of a solid base.

That even before the court he continued in his role—for instance, by explaining that the reason he never sought public office was that, at Athens, only a corrupt holder of public office would not lose his life in no time[2]—no doubt cost him a number of votes, perhaps a critical one: the majority against him was small, six in a court of five hundred and one. More precisely, the majority for finding him guilty. Between that verdict and the actual sentence he made a second, even more sarcastic speech: thus he argued that his punishment ought to consist in an honourable pension from the state.[3] After this, the majority for death was eighty-six.

I would add that, by calling himself a gadfly, he does admit that he acts contrary to convention in a stinging fashion, though he would not admit to outright illegality. In a sense, his refusal to escape after being sentenced to death was his last act of stinging; I shall say something about it below.[4] If I were to deliver more than six lectures in this course, I should include one on gadflies. In modern life, we might think of filibusters or such-like methods—devices which while still just within the law, come very near civil disobedience and can be just as effective.

A second fact which must be given its due weight is that some of his disciples, men like Alcibiades, did go far beyond reflection and debate and resorted to what, even now, most historians look on as destructive activity and treason. A contemporary analogy would be not some talkative academic circle with risky views nobody considers putting into practice, but a philosopher whose pupils under his inspiration—as they see it—will set fire to banks and maybe betray military installations to foreign powers. Socrates' judges were certainly influenced by what they considered very concrete consequences

---

[1] Plato, *Apology* 18.30 E ff.
[2] *Apology* 19.31 D f.   [3] *Apology* 26.36 A ff.   [4] See pp. 75 ff.

of his preaching. We must remember that it was not uncommon in antiquity for a master to be called to account for what his followers were doing. Socrates himself on occasion availed himself of this idea.[1] In the New Testament it is Jesus who has to explain why his disciples pluck corn on the Sabbath, or do not wash their hands before a meal.[2]

Thirdly, there had been very definite occasions in Socrates' career when he opposed the current trend in a degree hateful to a good many of his fellow-countrymen. Once some generals were to be collectively tried and finished; they had fallen from grace and the populace clamoured for their heads. Socrates, who happened to be a member of the court, stood out in opposing the illegal, collective proceedings.[3] The other incident occurred under the relatively short-lived tyranny of the Thirty, when he with others was given an order to arrest one of the enemies of the regime called Leon of Salamis. He, as he says, 'simply went home'; in other words he did nothing; he did not create a disturbance or even uselessly declare his refusal, he simply went home. The regime fell too soon for anything terrible to happen to him.[4]

On both occasions he risked his life and was lucky to get away with it. Moreover, both times the Athenians after a while sided with his view of the rights and wrongs of the affair. Nevertheless, it must have rankled that he took this brave, individualistic line. It cannot have militated in his favour at his trial in the minds of his judges.

Lastly, Socrates came dangerously near the proposition that, as the fruits of wrongdoing are bitter and no one would deliberately attract bitterness, there is no deliberate wrongdoing: any wrongdoing is in a sense unwitting and should be answered not with punishment but with instruction. He formu-

---

[1] Plato, *Euthyphro* 5.5 Af. Socrates, already indicted for corruption of the youth, asks Euthyphro—who prides himself on full knowledge of religious matters—to become his teacher. This will enable him to tell his accuser either to drop his charges or, if he still thinks Socrates' doctrines wrong, to bring to trial Euthyphro, 'my teacher, rather than me and charge him with corrupting the old'.
[2] Matthew 12.2, 15.2, Mark 2.24, 7.5. Luke differs. In the case of the Sabbath, the Pharisees reproach the disciples themselves (6.2)—though it is still Jesus who conducts the defence; and in the case of the meal, it is Jesus himself who omits the washing of hands (11.38).
[3] *Apology* 20.32 Aff., Xenophon, *Hellenica* 1.7.15, *Memorabilia* 1.1.18.
[4] *Apology* 20.32 Aff.

lated this doctrine before his judges with reference to corruption of youth,[1] but they must have seen (if they did not know
before) that it could easily be extended to murder, adultery,
robbery; and they would look upon it as a formidable threat to
the orderly running of a society—just as similar teachings are
looked upon today.

The problem ventilated again and again is why, when he lay
in prison under sentence of death and his friends offered to help
him escape and emigrate, he declined to do so. In answering
this puzzle we have to rely heavily on two works by Plato, the
Apology, which purports to transmit several addresses delivered
by Socrates during and after his trial, and the *Crito*, which
purports to transmit a conversation with a friend visiting him
in prison. The first thing one is struck by is the marvellous
blend of moral and practical considerations. Naturally, modern
exponents of Socrates' philosophy concentrate on the former and
I, too, shall do so. But let us note that they lose nothing of their
high tenor, indeed, gain in genuineness and depth, by the in-
clusion of the latter. For example, when he stresses the pain-
fulness of exile, the likelihood of being distrusted by his hosts
and the fear of being humiliated by awkward questions and
taunts,[2] it only enhances his humanity. Again, he is by now an
old man—seventy—and ready to go,[3] surely, a good feeling.

Of his moral arguments against falling in with his friends,
four may be listed—besides a motive of the utmost force
which, however, surfaces only in a speech before the court,[4] not
in his discussions with his would-be liberators: the consciousness that his death will ensure for him and his ideals a status
not achievable by any other means. I shall return to this
aspect,[5] but for the moment I propose to look at four arguments
he spells out.

First, his friends would be subject to penalties. As they are
influential, these might not be excessive; maybe they could be
avoided altogether. Still, he does not want to create difficulties
for them.[6] Second, by spending all his life at Athens, by
dwelling there under the protection of the laws, and by advis-
edly refusing in his defence speeches to propose exile as an

---

[1] *Apology* 13.25 E f. See Daube, *Sin, Ignorance and Forgiveness in the Bible*, 1960, pp. 21 f., 27.
[2] *Apology* 27.37 D, *Crito* 15.53 B ff.   [3] *Crito* 1.43 C; cp. 15.53 D f.
[4] *Apology* 29.38 E ff.   [5] See below, pp. 78 f.
[6] *Crito* 4.44 E ff., 15.53 B.

75

alternative to the death sentence, he agreed to abide by whatever the court would impose on him.[1] Thirdly a child must in the last resort suffer even the wrongful chastisement meted out by a parent; the city is his parent, so he must stay.[2] And fourthly, if he escaped he would be doing harm to the city and its laws, since the continued existence of the city is dependent on people yielding to the decisions of its courts.[3]

How does this attitude relate to his previous conduct? Escape would involve no violence. How is it more reprehensible than some of the things he had done before? I am not referring to his stand when the generals were to be illegally dispatched. In that case he had flouted no laws, indeed, it was the rest who avowedly set aside all regard for traditional rules.[4] But in the case of Leon of Salamis he had resisted an order from above. True, the order was arbitrary; he was, one might argue, resisting the tyrants enunciating it, not the laws of the state. But the verdict against him, in his eyes, was also quite unjust. In running away, it might be argued, he would be resisting, not the laws, but the arbitrary whims of those misconstruing them.[5] Moreover, in his speeches before the court he insists[6] that, even if formally requested to abstain from philosophizing with people and questioning them as to the meaning of their actions, he would go on with what he looks on as a divinely ordained mission; presumably he would go on even in the face of a decree debarring him from so doing. Once again it might be contended that such a prohibition was utterly unreasonable and wrong, not a true law, and in transgressing it he would be slighting the silly men who did not understand him, and not any genuine obligation. But again this excuse, at first sight at least, could be transferred to an escape from execution stupidly resolved on by the judges. Why does he feel so very differently in this situation?

One obvious difference is that whereas in the other situations he went on with his deviant plans in the interest of others, be it by conferring on them the benefits springing from his probing into human endeavour, be it by abstaining from injury as in the case of Leon of Salamis, in the present situation, if he

---

[1] *Crito* 14.52 Aff. [2] *Crito* 12.50 Eff.
[3] *Crito* 11.50 A f. For the last three reasons, see Jones, *The Law and Legal Theory of the Greeks*, 1956, pp. 1 f.
[4] See *e.g.* Xenophon, *Hellenica* 1.7.29.
[5] *Crito* 16.54 Bf. [6] *Apology* 17.29 Cff., 28.37 E f.

fled, the purpose would be to save himself. That is clearly one vital difference. Note that he does not reproach, indeed, gives praise to, his friends who are willing to help him break out:[1] they would be contravening the laws for the sake of another person.

A further difference is the distinction between ordinary laws and orders on the one hand, and the decision of an Athenian court resulting from what we would call due process on the other. To practise civil disobedience to ordinary laws and orders which violate your conscience is one thing; to practise it to the decision of a court is another. The latter enjoys a special, sanctity: once it is flouted the city cannot go on as an organized, coherent society.[2] After all, it was by then only a rather short time since feuds and all sorts of irregular settling of disputes had been replaced by orderly, democratic—or democratic-looking—procedures. Some of the most important plays of Aeschylus concern the gradual and painfully acquired institution of orderly courts.[3] Here, then, is a matter so sensitive that civil disobedience has no place.

Significantly, among the Noachian laws (the laws which according to rabbinical teaching were given after the Flood to the entire world, Jews and gentiles alike), one, in the opinion of some rabbis, was to establish courts of law.[4] Legal systems, the rabbis held, might differ in their rules—except for a very few necessary ones such as the prohibition of murder; the gentiles, that is, were free to evolve whatever systems they fancied. But to institute and respect courts enforcing no-matter-what body of rules, that, for one rabbinic school of thought at least, was an essential Noachian, you might say 'natural' commandment. Again, in much Western jurisprudence, especially the sector leaning on Austin, the sanction, the repression of wrong committed, counts as the central element, the heart, of a legal order;[5] a most understandable doctrine, considering the way the bulk of the population experiences the law. To some extent present-day international law, with its fairly recent endeavour to settle quarrels judicially, is comparable to the Athenian system of Socrates' time. A spurn-

---

[1] *Crito* 6.46 B.   [2] *Crito* 11.50 B.
[3] See my brother Benjamin Daube's *Zu den Rechtsproblemen in Aischylos' Agamemnon*, 1938, pp. 50 ff.   [4] Babylonian Sanhedrin 56 af.
[5] See *e.g.* two articles by Ebenstein and Cowan in 'Tribute to Kelsen', *California Law Review*, **59**, 1971, pp. 617 ff. and 683 ff.

ing of a decision of the Hague Court hurts the developing international regime more than disregard of some substantive rule.

If one were a Freudian, one would seek to find a factor in this special sanctity of court-decreed punishment coming from childhood experience. Socrates, or Plato who reports him, relieves us of this search, since he himself, as I mentioned, adverts to the city as a parent and his child-like duty to accept, therefore, even undeserved chastisement.[1] It is indeed a common phenomenon that the wildest child will none the less, when called upon to take his punishment, be ready to suffer; and I am sure that when Socrates transfers this attitude to his dilemma under sentence of death, he is giving expression to a widespread emotion among offenders, whether conscientious offenders or ordinary ones. The readiness to submit to judgement and penalties is astonishingly universal. Why a child should behave in the way he does it is not my task here to inquire; I single out two elements only. One—guilt, which primarily accompanies deeds the child feels are wrong but which spills over even into situations where he believes he has done right. The other—the fact that, as a rule, in the ultimate situation where the parent is about to inflict punishment for a misdeed, the sanctions in the event of resistance are particularly severe. What I mean is, if the child disobeys an order not to go out in the evening, the sanction may be a good thrashing; but if he then refuses the thrashing, the sanction might be an enormous beating-up plus being shut up in a dark room for two weeks and so on. So the verdict-and-punishment situation will be endowed with a peculiar respect. There are other important factors working in the same direction into which I shall not go.

How far Socrates' deliberations would stand up in a greatly changed setting I do not presume to answer. There may be periods when society is less endangered by disregard of a judicial verdict, or there may be a society containing groups so alienated that they are not concerned in any organized goings-on. In fact we may have to reckon with an even more extreme alternative, and here I come back to a motive of Socrates referred to earlier:[2] the attainment by a glorious death of apotheosis, final victory over all enemies, immortality of reputation. In conditions of mass de-humanization and extermination

---

[1] *Crito* 12.50 Eff.; see above, p. 76.   [2] See above, p. 75.

this motive may no longer be valid at all. It has been forcefully suggested[1] that whereas the traditional hero of former times dies for a cause, the modern hero of our day survives for it—the inmate of a concentration camp, for example, whose reward consists in remaining alive, and human, despite all pressure. Camus, Malamud, Solzhenitsyn write on this modern hero.

Maybe the rejection of Jesus by Judaism and the often found feeling among Jewry that Christianity is a life-denying religion are partly explicable on this basis. The two religions proceed from fundamentally different experiences. For whereas, on the whole, Christendom, up to recently at least, has been leading a civilized existence where a martyr's death makes sense, Jewry, on the whole, from well before the advent of Christianity, has been holding on in Camus' plague-stricken town, or in Malamud's or Solzhenitsyn's unending confinement, where the aim must be sheer existence and refusal to lose one's spirit. Note the typically Jewish joint attention to mind and body, indispensable in these conditions. And in these conditions the hero, who is anything but heroic in the old sense, who is simply a tenacious survivor, just barely preserving his outer and inner self, would escape if he could.

Allow me a comment in conclusion on a curious division of legal systems in the matter of treatment of escape from prison. In English law, and consequently in American law, it is punishable.[2] But in some other systems, like the German, it is not.[3] If, while escaping, you destroy a window, you are guilty of damage to property; and if you shoot a guard, well then, that is, of course, murder. But the escape as such is all right: suppose you just manage to climb over the wall, nothing will happen to you except, to be sure, that you may be recaptured. In English and American law, mere escape falls under the criminal law. To me, the German approach in this matter seems far more humane. It admits that the urge to be free is a natural quality of humans, so natural as to ground what I should almost describe as an inalienable right. To assist a prisoner to break out is punishable even in German law.[4] That, from the point of view of the state,

---

[1] By Des Pres, in *Encounter*, **37**, no. 3, September 1971, pp. 3 ff.
[2] See Perkins, *Criminal Law*, 2nd ed., 1969, pp. 500 ff.
[3] See Maurach, *Deutsches Strafrecht*, Besonderer Teil, 5th ed., 1969, pp. 654 ff.
[4] Not, of course, as aiding and abetting—for the prisoner's flight is no offence that could be aided and abetted—but as a wrong in its own

is perfectly justifiable. But the escaping prisoner himself does something anybody would—maybe should—want to do. It is up to the authorities to prevent him from doing so; it is not their business to hit him if he follows what must be one of the most elementary of man's instincts.

---

right; see Maurach op. cit., p. 655. Is a prisoner assisted to escape guilty of aiding and abetting his liberator? The German courts say No while—unreasonably (see Maurach, p. 656)—holding him guilty if he instigated the liberation. By a reform enacted in 1969, a negligent custodian is no longer punishable if the prisoner gets away: such punishability would interfere with the encouragement of more open forms of imprisonment—see Maurach, *Deutsches Strafrecht*, Besonderer Teil, Nachtrag, 1970, p. 53.

RELIGIOUS MINORITIES

1

In a lecture on religious minorities a prominent place may be assigned to the Jewish religion, which for several thousands of years has experienced this role. Some of the old rabbis however, would have denied this; they would have claimed that Judaism represents a majority.[1]

The reason is curious: in the Book of Exodus there is a prohibition which, no matter what its original meaning may have been, was used by the Jewish scholars in the period around the New Testament, as laying down that in disputes about religious matters, the majority of sages is to be followed.[2] That is how in fact important parts of their system were stabilized: we know of a number of controversies about points of theology or law settled by convoking a synod and taking a vote.[3] The majority rule, then, became a highly respected principle. To begin with, of course, it was meant to apply to disputes between different schools of thought within Judaism. But in course of time the rabbis found themselves questioned on this basis as to the relation between Judaism and heathen creeds. The questioners were not only educated gentiles but also their own disciples. Why, it was asked, if there was such magic virtue in a majority, should the Jews not become pagans? There were manifestly more pagans in the world than Jews. It was in refuting this argument that a number of rabbis felt driven to portray their religion as that of the majority.

A second-century example of how it could be done has come down to us. A famous sage, asked to express himself on the dilemma, contends that the worshippers of idols, and a large

---

[1] See Daube, *California Law Rev.*, **59**, 1971, pp. 792 ff.
[2] Exodus 23.2, Babylonian Baba Metzia 59 b, Hullin 11 a, Leviticus Rabba 4 on 4.1 f.
[3] E.g. Babylonian Shabbath 16 b.

variety of idols to boot, cannot possibly be regarded as a proper religious community; they are just so many individuals. Therefore, the servants of the one true God, the Jews, who are a united body, form an invincible majority, one that can never be outnumbered.[1]

However, that was of course a theory to allay the scruples of Jews worried by the awkward fact that the bulk of mankind, even of highly knowledgeable mankind, would have nothing to do with their religion. The reality with which Jewry has had to come to terms for several millennia is that it constitutes a tiny minority among an overwhelming majority believing otherwise.

I shall inspect two Old Testament works, Daniel and the Book of Esther. Then I shall present a contribution by Philo. After that I shall survey a rabbinic discussion, extending through many centuries, about a grievous problem a minority may have to face. This will be followed by some comments on the early Christians. In conclusion, I shall go somewhat beyond my subject and remark on an anti-war play by Aristophanes and on what happened to certain secret papers at Rome.

2

Daniel may be described as a veritable charter of civil disobedience by a religious minority.

Three chapters deal with the problem. One has regard to the Jewish dietary rules.[2] Daniel and three Jewish friends of his are among the handsome young men selected to serve as pages at the heathen king's court. They do not wish to eat the unclean food provided, though it is regarded by the royal servants as by far the most reliable nourishment for enhancing a boy's looks and well-being. It is noteworthy that, in this question, Daniel and his comrades do not simply resist the arrangements, and no really critical situation arises. What they do is: they persuade the chamberlain charged with looking after them to allow them a kasher, vegetarian diet for a trial period; in this way he himself is made to realize that this diet does them no harm, on the contrary, they excel their heathen colleagues in health and beauty. What would have happened if the chamberlain had not consented to their plan, we are not told, but the implication is that this question of correct food is not one for which one would lay down one's life or gravely endanger one's position.

---

[1] Leviticus Rabba 4 on 4.1 f.   [2] Daniel 1.

As is well-known, by New Testament times it had become established doctrine among the rabbis that under duress you are permitted, indeed, obliged, to transgress any ordinary commandment; it is only murder, gross sexual crimes and idolatry which you must never commit, even if your refusal will cost you your life.[1] The Book of Daniel dates at the latest from the first half of the second century BC, from the period, that is, when the Syrian king Antiochus Epiphanes cruelly persecuted the Jewish religion. The chapter I have just outlined distinctly foreshadows the rabbinic regulation met in later sources.

Things are very different in two subsequent incidents recorded in Daniel. The king orders an idol, an image, to be worshipped, under pain of death in the event of refusal.[2] Daniel's three friends are denounced for not doing as bidden and are summoned before the king. He tells them that if they persist in their course, they will be thrown into a fiery furnace. They reply that they will not budge: 'If it is so destined, our God whom we serve is able to deliver us from the burning furnace and out of thine hand; and if it is not so destined, be it known unto thee, even then we will not serve thy gods, nor worship the golden image which thou hast set up'.[3] The three men are thrown into the furnace, but miraculously they survive, whereupon the king issues a decree that from now they must remain unmolested, indeed, they must be honoured since they clearly have a powerful god.

Here then, we find civil disobedience carried to much greater lengths than in the chapter concerning food: the resisters will die rather than commit idolatry. Again, fully consistent with the later, rabbinical doctrine to which I have adverted. Idolatry must in no circumstances be committed.

Similarly, in the third chapter here relevant,[4] the king asks to be recognized as a god, and all his subjects must address their prayers to him and no one else. Daniel stands out. Unconditional civil disobedience is here incumbent on him. He is cast into a lion's den—much to the king's grief because the king likes him. The lion miraculously spares him, and the king now ordains that Daniel's god must be acknowledged and feared by all.

---

[1] Babylonian Sanhedrin 74 a, Jerusalemite Sanhedrin 21 b.
[2] Daniel 3.   [3] Daniel 3.17f.
[4] Daniel 6. Whereas in chapters 1 and 3 the king is Nebuchadnezzar, here it is Darius.

It is astonishing that this Book, written, or at least edited, in an epoch of virulent persecution by the heathens and considerable revolutionary activism by the Jews, shows no trace of violent resistance. In the matter of food, Daniel and his friends manage to get around the law or convention governing life at the court by clever, thoughtful negotiation with the official administering this ressort. In the other cases they simply refrain from what, in their eyes, is a mortal sin, idolatry. Though the likelihood is they will die as a result, the possibility of fighting does not occur to them, is not so much as hinted at. No one could be more peaceable, indeed, courteous; not a cross word, an atmosphere totally removed from, for instance, the Books of the Maccabees, where we find the tyrant addressed 'Thou cursed miscreant'.[1] Indeed, in yet another chapter of Daniel,[2] the hero saves not only the lives of himself and his three Jewish comrades but also those of the heathen wise men of Babylon.

Let me insert here that there is among scholars a strange insensitivity to the kind of difference I have just mentioned. 'The martyrs of II Maccabees', we are told by a leading authority,[3] 'act with the courage and piety of Daniel and his three companions in refusing to compromise with paganism'; he refers specifically to the story of Razis,[4] and he goes on to draw further parallels. As for Daniel, I think I have said enough about the sweet manner in which the Jewish heroes meet their antagonists; as the king comes to the lion's den into which Daniel was thrown the previous day, Daniel receives him with the words, 'O King, live forever'.[5] Razis, surrounded by hostile troops, threw himself from the wall. Now I quote: 'Still alive, however, he got up in a fury of anger and ran, with blood pouring from him, right through the crowds; then, standing on a steep rock, he tore out his bowels, taking both his hands to them, and flung them at the crowds'. This is no more like Daniel than Günther Grass is like Jane Austen.

Daniel is an apocalyptic work, in fact, the earliest work of this nature preserved to us. I would risk the generalization that the apocalyptic literature, all of it, has its setting in that part of the

---

[1] II Maccabees 7.9.   [2] Daniel 2.
[3] Brownlee, s.v. Maccabees, Books of, *The Interpreter's Dictionary of the Bible*, 3, 1962, p. 209.
[4] II Maccabees 14.37 ff.   [5] Daniel 6.21.

nation subscribing to non-violent conduct. The story of Judith, not very distant in time from Daniel, is violent: it is not apocalyptic. The lady, in order to save her people, goes into the enemy's camp, makes herself agreeable to the general, gets him to drink himself senseless at a jolly dinner, accompanies him to his bedroom, takes his sabre and cuts his head off. No eschatological imaginings here. Again, the First and Second Books of Maccabees celebrate the violent insurrection of Jewry. Their message of armed resistance is unmistakable. They play no music of the future, they are not apocalyptic treatises. Daniel is apocalyptic, and it depicts the tamest conceivable behaviour on the part of its heroes.

Apocalyptic writing concentrates on the end-time dissolution of history in a way the initiated can foresee. There will be the most gruesome wonders, paradoxical happenings, fearful inflictions on the wicked, rescues of the saintly, but all these phases can be exactly predicted by means of special insights and calculations. 'Apocalypsis' means 'revelation of secrets': no doubt it is precisely because the believers in these fantastic pictures 'knew', i.e. had the fullest certainty and the fullest relief from present burdens in their spiritual life, that, in real life, they could take things peaceably, abstaining from wrong, but not forcing issues. Two other factors may be mentioned. The very uninhibited wildness of the apocalyptic dream would make it less necessary to be mundanely efficient, would be a substitute for, so to speak, acting out. Furthermore, there is the profound pessimism entertained by many of an apocalyptic turn of mind with regard to anything pertaining to this world: 'O thou Earth, what hast thou brought forth if the mind is sprung from the dust as every other created thing! It had been better if the dust itself had even been unborn, so that the mind might not have come into being from it.'[1] In these circumstances, outward-directed action is futile.

However, the dominant and universal motive is the absolute conviction that the denouement is coming about in accordance with an inevitable plan which its author has disclosed to his servants. For them, to stand and wait. This goes through all apocalyptic preaching. If you take the thirteenth chapter of Mark, all around the pious ones there will be the most horrific events. There will be earthquakes and famines, nations shall

---

[1] II Esdras 7.62 f.

rise against nations, brother shall betray brother to death, father shall betray son, children shall betray parents, and the persecutions of the faithful will reach terrible heights. Yet, what are they enjoined to do? They are enjoined to maybe defend themselves by pleading when they are caught. But they are not told to intervene in any way by action. The stars of heaven shall fall, angels will do all sorts of things, but they must simply be good and not fall away; aside from this, all they must do is watch and pray and flee to the mountains; no participation whatever as the final, awful scene unrolls itself.

A few more illustrations. The Book of Revelation, despite its vials full of the wrath of God,[1] its horsemen,[2] the war of Gog and Magog,[3] requires patience and faithfulness unto death.[4] Enoch describes the blessings in store for the saints and the overthrows in store for the sinners. For the present, however, your task is to observe,[5] to be steadfast,[6] to be hopeful,[7] to walk in the paths of righteousness and not in those of violence.[8] The Syriac Apocalypse of Baruch bids you remain untroubled and patient—the judgement will assuredly come at the appointed time;[9] and II Esdras warns you that 'Thy haste may not exceed that of the Most High'.[10]

It is important, obviously, to realize this essential connection of apocalypse and civil disobedience. I cannot here go into the manifold results that emerge. One of them is that the assignment of the quiet and impetuous portions of Daniel to different authors turns out quite unwarranted. (It is indeed mostly rejected nowadays on other grounds.)[11] To a modern reader, the quiet, firm conduct of Daniel and his companions in the narrative sections and the grotesque visions seem to have nothing to do with one another, indeed, seem to be definitely inconsistent. But these two moods are of the very nature of the apocalyptic approach. The Book of Baruch is still generally considered to be composite.[12] Whether it is or not, it is unsound to use as

---

[1] Revelation 15.7ff. [2] Revelation 6.1ff. [3] Revelation 20.8.
[4] Revelation 2.2f., 10. [5] Enoch 2f. [6] Enoch 5.4, 92.2.
[7] Enoch 96.1, 104.2. [8] Enoch 91.19. [9] II Baruch 22f.
[10] II Esdras 4.34.
[11] See Frost, s.v. Daniel, *The Interpreter's Dictionary of the Bible*, I, 1962. p. 764.
[12] See Tedesche, s.v. Baruch, Book of, *The Interpreter's Dictionary of the Bible*, I, 1962, p. 764.

argument the fact[1] that one part recommends submission to and prayer for the Babylonian ruler whereas another predicts delivery from oppression. The latter part shows the typical apocalyptic blend of restraint now and full blast in the future: 'Suffer patiently the wrath that is come upon you for God, for thine enemy hath persecuted thee. But shortly thou shalt see his destruction and shalt tread upon their necks'.[2]

May I just add that our assessment of the Dead Sea people, the Essenes, the Zealots, and their mutual relations will be greatly affected. The War Scroll, 'the war of the sons of light and the sons of darkness'—my hunch is that the group that produced this work was far removed from any practical plotting against whatever overlords may have governed the country. As far as I know, no weapons have been found at their site: bowls, plates, cups, jars, the excavators have come up with—not weapons.[3] The Manual of Discipline names a fair number of communal offices and jobs, not one of which with a martial connotation. 'They were holy men and holy warriors', the experts assert.[4] I wonder as to the second half of this characterization. Again: 'the sect probably defended the monastery bravely, so that the enemy set fire to it'. This is possible even if, generally, they were pacific. But who knows? They may, for example, have fired the monastery themselves.[5]

3

The Book of Esther deserves special attention. It contains several instances of civil disobedience, and though in themselves they are not perhaps momentous, in its final version, which lies before us, the work is a piece of political indoctrination, with a veritable programme. This tightly written story, that is, comprises quite a few layers: myth, celebrating a war between different deities, history, recounting a rescue of a Jewry

---

[1] See Whitehouse, in Charles, *The Apocrypha and Pseudepigrapha of the Old Testament*, I, 1913, p. 570.
[2] I Baruch 4.25.
[3] The site was re-occupied after the end of the Dead Sea sect: any finds from the latter strata are, of course, irrelevant.
[4] Betz, s.v. Dead Sea Scrolls, *The Interpreter's Dictionary of the Bible*, I, 1962, p. 794.
[5] The last defender of Masada set fire to the palace before committing suicide: Josephus, *War* 7.9.2.397. He did, however, belong to an implacably belligerent faction.

from dire danger, Wisdom, presenting certain types of behaviour for emulation or avoidance, and—on top of it all—propaganda addressed to a country which harbours Jews.[1] By virtue of this last twist the Book becomes an attempt to convince the host government that it has more to gain from an orderly taxation of Jewish commerce than from a once-for-all expropriation and destruction. That is why the most dramatic scene, where Queen Esther unmasks the villain Haman, culminates—at first sight incongruously—in a dry, economic argument;[2] that is why the tale concludes—at first sight anticlimactically—with a levy jointly devised by the king and his Jewish prime minister Mordecai.[3] Seeing that there is here a well thought out scheme as to how host country and Jewry should interact, it is worthwhile to look into the modes and effects of resistance depicted.

The Persian queen Vashti's recalcitrance in the very first chapter I discussed in my opening lecture:[4] she declines her husband's command to display her charms before his assembled nobles. For this upholding of her royal and (more generally) feminine dignity she loses her throne, and a decree is passed establishing male dominance throughout the princely courts of the realm. Her punishment is not barbarous; it is only subsequent elaborations of the narrative which represent her as being beheaded. Still it is serious enough to convey the moral that hers is not the ideal womanly attitude. The work presents a worse type and a better one. The wicked Haman's wife confirms anything he does or says: she shares in his utter downfall. Esther, the Jewess who is crowned in the place of the too proud Vashti, does everything to please her husband, and precisely in this way obtains a position of enormous influence. As far as Jewish-gentile relations are concerned, the import of her conduct is that a

---

[1] See Daube, *Jewish Quarterly Rev.*, **37**, 1946, pp. 139 ff. The wisdom element has been brilliantly established by Talmon, *Vetus Testamentum*, **13**, 1963, pp. 419 ff. Like many discoverers, he is one-sided and has no eyes for the other strata. Moreover, he exaggerates the typology: for example, Mordecai is a less than perfect incarnation of prudent, austere tight-lippedness—giving away his provenance to his ill-wishers, Esther 3.4.

[2] Esther 7.4. It is so incongruous that translators and commentators have never ceased getting rid of it.

[3] Esther 10.1. It is so anticlimactic that commentators incline to throw it out as spurious. Why anyone should have bothered to append it they do not stop, or stoop, to consider.

[4] See above, The Women of the Bible and Greece, pp. 14 ff.

Jewess will happily unite with a gentile man, at least with one of exceptional rank, and will fall in with his gentile customs. The rabbis seek to represent Esther as faithful to Jewish practices.[1] But there is no remark to this effect in the original Book. Indeed, it is an essential part of the story that, for a good while, she keeps the king in the dark as to her Jewish affiliation[2]—which would not be possible were she to insist on Jewish observances. She is no Daniel. A further detail agrees with this. The work attaches high value to a people's language;[3] and the decree just mentioned provides that in a bilingual marriage the husband's tongue is to prevail. Esther evidently bows to this ruling; submission in this matter is, then, recommended to Jewesses marrying out—a teaching greatly at variance with that of the Book of Nehemiah.[4]

An instance of civil disobedience by a Jew sets in motion the main course of events.[5] The king makes Haman his chief minister and ordains that everybody has to bow down whenever he appears. Mordecai refuses to do so. We are not told about his motivation. It looks—especially when we bear in mind the opening chapter about Queen Vashti—as if it were primarily a matter of dignity and pride. While Haman is a descendant of the Amalekite kings, Mordecai belongs to a noble Jewish house: Saul's father is his ancestor.[6] He would not recognize Haman as his superior. In later additions to the narrative his intent is assimilated to that of Daniel: he has religious scruples, such worshipful homage ought to be reserved for God.[7] Significantly, Josephus takes over this reinterpretation which, in an explanation of Mordecai's refractoriness to a Roman public, is easier to represent as part of the general Jewish system.[8] In the

---

[1] The apocryphal Prayer of Esther, 17 (in the LXX, Esther 14.28), Esther Rabba 2 on 2.11.
[2] Apart from the function of this concealment in the plot, Mordecai, who advises Esther not to tell, evidently feels that if she did tell, the anti-Semites would be alerted and a valuable means of entrapping them be lost.
[3] Esther 1.22, 3.12, 7.9. The saving edict of 7.9 is sent out also in a Jewish version.
[4] Nehemiah 13.24.   [5] Esther 3.1ff.   [6] Esther 3.2, 2.5.
[7] Prayer of Mordecai 5ff. (in the LXX, Esther 13.12ff.): 'Thou knowest, Lord, that it was not in insolence or pride or vainglory that I did not bow before Haman, but that I might not set the glory of man above the glory of God, and I will bow before none save before thee'.
[8] Josephus, *Jewish Antiquities* 11.6.5.210, 8.230. More details below, p. 91.

actual Book of Esther, theological stringency of this kind, while perfectly conceivable, probably plays a secondary part.

Haman resolves on a very extreme course.[1] He decides to wipe out the entire Jewry of the Persian empire and appropriate all their wealth. He wins the king's approval by dwelling on the separateness of Jewry, its life under its own laws, its contempt for the laws proclaimed by the government. In the nick of time, however, the new queen, Esther, reveals her nationality to the king and convinces him that Haman's plan, besides affronting and endangering her person, would do grave harm to the king's finances. So the Jews are saved and Haman perishes.

It is noteworthy that the focus is on the daring of a prominent Jew. As for the mass of his co-religionists, for one thing, they would presumably do as they are bidden, and for another, if any of them ventured not to, he would be dealt with in summary fashion. Only a figure of the highest standing has any chance. On the other hand, precisely on account of his rank, his resistance spells the gravest danger to the whole community. Even an ordinary Jew's insubordination is apt to be visited on the rest; a man like Mordecai rouses all the accumulated ill-will. In this case, the community seems to accept his risky procedure without blaming him. Frequently, such perilous high-mindedness is resented by those who may be drawn into the resulting upheaval. As we shall see in the last lecture, the Israelites in Egypt found Moses' provocation of Pharaoh irresponsible.[2] No doubt Mordecai's connection with the palace inspires confidence that the affair will end well.

In the end his brinkmanship is vindicated. The king, enlightened by Esther, encourages the Jews to arm themselves and do away with any who dare attack them.[3] Their enemies are declared in the wrong, and such violence as is necessary to repel them turns into rightful self-defence.

The message to the gentile world is that the Jews should be

---

[1] The psychology is extraordinarily subtle. Left alone, Haman might never have noticed Mordecai's behaviour. It was other courtiers who resented the latter's not joining them in the prescribed display of servility and who, when he paid no heed to their reprimands, drew Haman's attention to the case—at the same time informing him of what Mordecai himself had told them, his nationality.

[2] Exodus 5.21. See below, Aspirants to Statehood, p. 126.

[3] Esther 8.11 ff.

left to practice their strange customs and lead their lives un-molested and, indeed, without having to submit to others as their betters. Mordecai replaces Haman as chief minister: Jewish well-being, it is demonstrated, will work best for the gentiles. The Jews—or rather, trade in general, Jewish or gentile—can be taxed, and that should benefit everybody.[1]

It is interesting that later Jewish elaborations of the narrative add to the anti-Semitic case: the king, while still siding with Haman, points out that Jewry's nonconformity spoils the con-solidation and security of the empire he wishes to achieve.[2] Josephus largely adopts this argument, no doubt often facing him in debate with Romans.[3] There is good sense in making the king start out from this position: his transformation into a protector of Jewry thereby becomes all the more impressive. I have already mentioned that, according to Josephus, Mordecai's refusal to pay obeisance to Haman springs from the purist notion that the act would be inconsistent with the exclusive worship of God. Josephus refers to Mordecai's 'wisdom and native laws'.[4] The native laws are obviously those of the Pen-tateuch. By wisdom Josephus may well mean a consideration acceptable to his gentile public too, and exemplified by two Spartan envoys of whom Herodotus tells us:[5] when asked to prostrate themselves before Xerxes, they declared that, as digni-fied free men, they would die rather than do so before any mortal being.[6]

---

[1] Josephus tells the story of a tax directly after that of Esther: *Jewish Antiquities* 11.7.1.297. It is possible that somehow the tax at the end of the Book of Esther is at the back of his mind.

[2] Letter of Artaxerxes 4ff. (in the LXX, Esther 13.4ff.).

[3] *Jewish Antiquities* 11.6.6.217ff.

[4] *Jewish Antiquities* 11.6.5.210.

[5] Herodotus 7.136. The envoys were scapegoats of a sort: volunteers, handing themselves over to Xerxes in order to atone for a crime the Spartans had committed long before against Persian ambassadors. Xerxes, however, declined their offer and spared them.

[6] In Babylonian Sanhedrin 74 b it is asked whether Esther, publicly marrying an idolator, was not in breach of Jewish norms of conduct. One rabbi justifies her by remarking that 'she was soil of the world', *qarqaᶜ ᶜolam hayetha*. I am mystified. All I know is that the explanation given by the commentators is unconvincing: Esther was merely passive. For one thing, if this were meant, 'soil' would do. Why 'soil of the world'? Sometimes one senses the further implication that she experi-enced no pleasure—a sound puritanical exculpation but not one attri-butable to an early fourth-century scholar.

4

In most countries where suicide is taken off the criminal code, the abetting of it is not.[1] Suppose three persons, intending to protest in conspicuous fashion against a war, build a pyre in the centre of a town, ascend it, pour petrol on it, set it on fire and thus burn to death. Is it civil disobedience? Is it violence? I guess some authorities would rule out the former alternative because the three do not follow up their demonstration by presenting themselves for punishment.[2]

Philo makes an outstanding—I am tempted to say, awesome —contribution to this domain. In AD 39-40, as the Jews of Jabneh destroyed an altar to Caligula, the latter, enraged, ordered a statue of himself to be introduced into the Temple. A vast concourse of Jews, men, women and children, now came to the headquarter of the governor Petronius, to beseech him not to proceed with the sacrilege. To go by Philo,[3] their spokesmen assured him that they had no intention of fighting. The Romans might mow them down if they liked (a fairly recent incident[4] was proof that this offer was not just rhetoric); there would be no armed resistance. Actually, they added (and this is the part I am concerned with), rather than live with the Temple desecrated, they themselves would seek extinction: the men would first kill their families and then crown their deadly deeds by killing themselves.

In wartime, with all hope of warding off a bitter, merciless enemy gone, extreme measures of this description had been taken before and have been taken since: they would constitute an ultimate defiance, depriving the conqueror of his conquest. They are now approved, now disapproved. Josephus contains impassioned argumentation for and against—and in between.[5] Polybius finds in them an element 'august and admirable'.[6] Livy calls the self-annihilation of the city of Astapa 'a barbarous, savage outrage'.[7]

---

[1] See *Wharton's Criminal Law and Procedure* by Anderson, **1**, 1957. p. 236, Williams, *The Sanctity of Life and the Criminal Law*, 1957, pp. 296 ff.
[2] See above, The Women of the Bible and Greece, pp. 4 f., Prophets and Philosophers, pp. 67, 75 ff.
[3] *Embassy to Gaius* 229 ff.
[4] Josephus, *War* 2.9.3.173 f, *Antiquities* 18.3.1.58 f.
[5] *War* 3.8.4.355 ff., 7.8.6.320 ff.   [6] 16.33.4: *semnon kai thaumasion*.
[7] 28.22.5: *facinus foedum ac ferum*.

Philo, however, takes an entirely different line. He portrays the threatened act as anything but martial. The spokesmen, he tells us, explained to Petronius that, by carrying out this massacre, they would prove faithful both to the Emperor and their religion. They would be faithful to the former, that is, in removing themselves as obstacles to his project; and to the latter, in not being there to tolerate the intolerable evil. The massacre is thus represented as hardly even civil disobedience, certainly not a crime of violence. On the contrary, it is said to reflect the Jews' 'reverence of the Emperor'.[1]

How does he come to propound this astonishing construction? For I take it that, at least in this refined form, the idea is due to him rather than to the people pleading with the governor. Some inspiration he probably derived from the sphere of individual suicide. In general, if you do away with yourself under duress—otherwise you will be tortured to death or your family will be penalized or your property confiscated—you do not profess to cherish the person from whom the duress emanates. Yet if that person was the Emperor, such a profession was not unusual. Indeed, you might stress your eagerness to quit life because the beloved figure no longer smiled on you, or because you sensed a desire on his part to have you gone. Tacitus considers it noteworthy that Petronius Arbiter, driven to suicide by Nero, refused to flatter him in his last will.[2] But we need not look that far. Philo quotes a letter—whether it is genuine or not does not here matter—in which Herod Agrippa I, King of Judaea, humbly begged his benefactor Caligula to withdraw his order, adding that if the Emperor resented this request, would he please bid the king 'get out of the way'.[3]

Still, it must have been a quite extraordinary stimulus that caused Philo to transfer this stance to mass-slaughter of innocents culminating in mass-suicide of the survivors. As far as I can see, nowhere else is such a bloodbath provided with the veneer of good, deferential citizenhood. The explanation is that,

---

[1] *Pros ton autokratora eulabeia.*   [2] *Annals* 16.19.

[3] *Ekpodon gignomai.* A certain aspect of this proposal I am discussing in The Linguistics of Suicide, in *Philosophy and Public Affairs*, 2, 1972. Agrippa, unless the order was withdrawn, found himself in the same insoluble, 'horned', dilemma on a personal level as the Jewish community was in as a public body. He could bear neither betraying his nation by condoning the order nor incurring Caligula's ill-will for contradicting him: *Embassy to Gaius* 327.

when he heard of the incident at Jabneh, Caligula's order and the attempts to influence Petronius, he was at Rome,[1] heading a Jewish delegation from Alexandria to supplicate Caligula with regard to difficulties there. He now made plans to raise the matter of the statue as well; and he had to devise a manner of presentation that would go down well with the Emperor. Hence the unique dressing-up of the fearful resolve.

Josephus's two accounts[2] depict the Jewish petitioners of the governor as far less prone to self-denial. They are ready to be wiped out by the Romans. But they do not affirm that they will not oppose them, nor do they announce a self-immolating massacre. That an uprising was rather likely emerges from other passages in Philo's own work[3]—not to mention Tacitus.[4] On the other hand, Agrippa's letter just adverted to does envisage a wholesale butchering of families followed by suicide in the event of insult to the sanctuary. (The elaborate interpretation of the step is not, however, here repeated.) Evidently, the colouring of these events and proposals would vary according to the public to whom they were retailed. The prospective public of Philo was a very special one.

His analysis deserves a closer look. Here was a collision between the secular authority and the sacred. He was an accomplished jurisprudent and knew that commonly, where two norms or systems conflict, the solution will be by means either of ranking or of distinguishing. By means of ranking: one of the two is assigned precedence so as to nullify the other. In the USA, a state law infringing the federal constitution is struck down. By means of distinguishing: the range of one or each of the two is circumscribed so as to arrive at separate fields of application. The first amendment lays down that no law shall abridge freedom of speech. Expediency and morality do call for such laws. A compromise long favoured was to hold that the first amendment did not extend to laws directed against a clear and present danger of serious harm, or against speech so obscene as to be unworthy of protection.[5]

In the case Philo had to deal with, the method of distinction would not do. Caligula's order was unambiguous; it would have been foolish to credit it with an innocuous meaning, say, to

---

[1] *Embassy to Gaius* 186ff.

[2] *War* 2.10.3.102ff., *Antiquities* 18.8.2.263ff.

[3] *Embassy to Gaius* 280, for instance.   [4] *Histories* 5.9.

[5] See Sinclair, *California Law Rev.*, **57**, 1969, pp. 1257ff.

pretend that it envisaged a spiritual statue, not a concrete one. Equally unambiguous was the Jewish tenet debarring an idol from the Temple. There had been many costly struggles in its defence. It was indeed an absolute, so no *modus vivendi* was conceivable on the basis of the order as it stood. That would necessitate a genuine, essential modification. What Agrippa in his letter tells about Tiberius[1]—obviously for Caligula to imitate—is designed to show that the chief purpose of the order, public homage to Caligula, could be achieved without arousing Jewish animosity. Pilate, Agrippa reminds him, put up in Herod's old palace at Jerusalem shields dedicated to the Emperor. The Jews were incensed. Whereupon Tiberius had the offending objects erected at Caesarea: 'thus both aims were safeguarded, the honour of the Emperor and the privileges of the city'.

What is fascinating is that Philo in this particular section (there are others where he speaks differently, but I am focussing on how he handled this acute dilemma) does not refer to the other method either. That is to say, he does not declare religious law to rank higher than the Emperor's. The very reason the grave is the only way out if the order remains in force is that both are to be respected. Alive, the Jews cannot manage this. But they can disappear, thus refraining (for the sake of religion) from admitting the image and at the same time rendering possible (for the sake of their duty as citizens) its installation over their dead bodies. Religious law and imperial law are here treated as both equally inviolable, both equally prized higher than life. The Emperor could complain of no slight in this evaluation.

And yet, Philo is a Jew *sans peur et sans reproche*. That in the end his religion is the measure of all things comes out clearly in what he sees as the ultimate warranty for his people becoming mass-slayers of their families and themselves: that God will not blame them. He is, of course, deeply aware of the fearful nature of the plan. Whatever he may have thought of suicide, the extermination of your nearest and dearest would ordinarily be a heinous offence. In the circumstances, it is justified as the only salvation from flouting either the will of God or the will of Caligula. But what, basically, does it mean that it is justified? 'God himself could not blame us', the spokesmen are made to

---

[1] *Embassy to Gaius* 299 ff.

exclaim, for thus upholding both loyalties. There is no doubt where, for Philo, supreme authority lies.

A question which might arise in our minds is as to the willingness or unwillingness of the wives and children to play the role allotted to them. For that matter, even some men might be too fond of life to approve of the desperate scheme. This problem does not engage ancient thinkers overmuch. It was largely taken for granted that the big decisions were made by the men, wives and children going along with them.[1] It did not, to be sure, always fully work out. Josephus escaped from such a scene after all his companions but one had bravely killed one another,[2] and even at Masada two women with five children survived the general ruin, hiding out in an aqueduct.[3] By contrast, when the last Sicarii were extradited to the Romans,[4] their families, including the young children, remained firm under the most terrible tortures and refused to acknowledge the Emperor as their lord.

The Jewish spokesmen before Petronius, in setting out the details of their contemplated action, use exalted language. Indeed, Philo has them draw attention to it: 'For the tragic vocabulary is needed for those who suffer tragic misfortunes'. It is possible to identify the source Philo has in mind. The spokesmen grieve at having to become *paidophontai*, 'child-killers'. This provides the clue. The allusion is to the Euripidean Heracles (or rather, *a* Euripidean Heracles, for Euripides brought him on the stage in more than one play). Heracles killed his children by Megara. In Hercules Furens, we find *haima paidophonon*, 'the blood of children killed'.[5] Euripides may be even closer to Philo in a work lost to us. Philo is fond of Euripides. There is a speech of Heracles which he quotes not fewer than four times;[6] once in a context relevant to the present one—namely, where he teaches that the good man is free in being unafraid of death and other external blows.[7] 'And, therefore, he will not obey just anyone who gives him orders, even though he menaces him with outrage and tortures and

---

[1] But see, for example, above, The Women of Rome, pp. 35 f.

[2] Josephus, *War* 3.8.7.391.   [3] Josephus, *War* 7.9.1.398 f.

[4] Josephus 7.10.1.409 ff; see below, p. 101.   [5] 1201.

[6] *Allegorical Interpretation* 3.202, *Joseph* 78, That Every Good Man is Free 25, 99.

[7] *That Every Good Man is Free* 25. Translation by Colson, *Philo* (*Loeb Classical Library*), 9, 1941, p. 25.

threats however dreadful, but will openly and boldly defy him thus:[1] "Roast and consume my flesh, and drink thy fill Of my dark blood: for sooner shall the stars Go 'neath the earth and earth go up to heaven Than thou shalt from my lips meet fawning word" '. A few paragraphs before,[2] he cites this line from the same poet: 'What man who minds not death can be a slave ?'

5

Well before the beginning of our era Jewish law had arrived at the doctrine that if you come upon a man who is about to murder another man, then, provided there is no other possibility of saving the victim, you should kill the attacker.[3] Say, you turn a corner and see some nasty chap aiming his flick-knife at a child: in default of a milder way out, you draw your Browning and shoot. This principle was formulated mainly for relations within the state in more or less settled times. If an occupying foreign power was bent on murdering people, it would have been sheer self-immolation — and mostly hopeless — to act upon it. Just imagine: a brutal governor sets about rounding up twenty or a hundred or two thousand people. You were not required to attempt to stab or strangle him or the execution squads. In fact, the main problem if the occupying power proceeded to indiscriminate slaughter was unfortunately quite different: not whether there was an obligation to step in but, how far, should they order you to participate in their designs, you might go along with them, and where you must draw the line.

It goes without saying that, if no frightful retribution is to be expected, you must never do a persecutor's bidding which involves a transgression of Jewish law or morality. But what if retribution is certain, and above all, what if the persecutor requires a transgression on pain of death ? After a good deal of deliberation, by New Testament times a large body of opinion was in favour of admitting that a person threatened with death if he declined to carry out an order could or even should obey — unless he was ordered to shed blood, to perform an outrageous sexual crime, or to commit idolatry. The exceptions are momentous. If, for example, a Roman captain ordered a Jew to put to death a fellow-Jew for some reason good enough in the

---

[1] Here begins the quotation from Euripides.
[2] *That Every Good Man is Free* 22; cp. Plutarch, *Moralia* 34 B.
[3] Mishnah Sanhedrin 8.7.

captain's eyes, the Jew so ordered would have to let himself be killed rather than comply.[1]

Civil disobedience is clearly a second-best. As I stated before, ordinarily, your duty is active intervention to save a prospective victim of murder. This cannot be expected in cases like that just posed. But at least civil disobedience is insisted on, even should it cost your life. There are limits to self-preservation; among them that you must not kill even if you are killed for this omission.

There was an even more tragic situation; one which perenially arises for persecuted minorities—namely, where the threat is not merely to an individual Jew, but to an entire group. One problem in particular formed the subject of much earnest discussion and rule-making among the rabbinical authorities from the first century of our era onwards. How far may a community —a city, a congregation—give in to an alien, oppressive regime which wants a member handed over for execution and declares that if the community does not obey, it will be wiped out?[2] This fearful dilemma is peculiarly familiar from the second world war. An act of sabotage is committed in a village, and early next morning the mayor receives a message from the commandant: 'I request you immediately to hand over two villagers of your choice for public hanging. If you do not do so by 11 o'clock, I shall send in a detachment and have all the inhabitants machine-gunned'. Or again, in a concentration camp, the Jewish leaders are ordered to collect within twenty-four hours five hundred boys between fourteen and seventeen for an extermination transport—if they fail to do so, the entire camp will be sent to Auschwitz.

In the earliest treatment the rabbis came to the conclusion that even if it means total extinction, such an order may never be followed. A city or congregation must allow itself to be obliterated rather than give away a single member to be killed. The duty of civil disobedience under this ruling is quite unconditional, and it was adhered to for a considerable period.

However, when in the first half of the second century the emperor Hadrian with difficulty defeated the revolt of Bar-

---

[1] Babylonian Sanhedrin 74 a, Jerusalemite Sanhedrin 21 b.
[2] See Daube, *Collaboration with Tyranny in Rabbinic Law*, 1965. The principal texts are Mishnah Terumoth 8.11f., Tosephta Terumoth 7.20, Jerusalemite Terumoth 46 b, Genesis Rabba 94 on 46.26f., Leviticus Rabba 19 on 15.25, John 11.46ff.

Kokhba and thereupon instituted a fierce persecution of Judaism in Palestine, the uncompromising stand became very precarious. Hadrian made it a capital crime to practice or teach the Jewish religion. As a result, a great many people became liable to the death penalty; and the Roman government again and again threatened a community with annihilation if they did not extradite, say, a rabbi who had given instruction or a pious man who had circumcised his son. Things came to such a head that if the ruling never to comply had continued to be observed, it would have led to the complete physical disappearance of Palestinian Jewry within a short time.

The leading rabbis assembled for a secret synod and a majority held that a mitigation of the old, unconditional prohibition was needed. A minority stood out, but the majority resolved as follows: if the regime asks for an unnamed, unspecified man, say, 'By this evening you deliver a citizen—to be killed in retaliation for an act of sabotage committed in the vicinity of the town', then even if refusal entails the end of the entire community, the request must be declined. A request for an unspecified victim means that humans are treated like cattle: anyone will do, the authorities just want to kill a subject—or two or three—no matter who it may be. In no circumstances can such an utterly immoral plan be accepted. An additional consideration against it is that the choice of the victim, however it were made—even if by lot or by relying on volunteers— would be the affair of the community and would undermine the mutual trust and cohesiveness within. By contrast, if the government asks for an identified person, Rabbi X, to execute otherwise they will expunge the community, then the request should be acceded to—though it means, of course, the handing over of a particularly valuable and wonderful member. At least, in this case, the government has a quarrel with a particular individual. The quarrel may be evil and thoroughly unjustified, but at least the beginnings of morality are there because humans are treated as humans, and not like cattle. And, of course, the government chooses the victim, not the community.

This less extreme solution, then, cut down civil disobedience in this area to manageable proportions. It is noteworthy that, very likely, the same synod which voted for a mitigated resistance in the case of a wholesale threat to a community reaffirmed the individual's obligation to let himself be slaughtered rather than obey a command to slaughter a fellow-being.

Some decades later, when the persecution had abated, the concession made by the secret synod was more or less revoked by further rabbinical decisions. Now it was laid down that a member of the community may be handed over only if he has in fact committed a crime which by general, what we call 'natural' law standards, could be regarded as deserving death. This was subsequently modified so as to admit extradition also of one who needlessly perpetrates a crime capital only by the ordinances of the regime. There is a moving rabbinic responsum from 17th century Poland.[1] A congregation was threatened because a member accused of the theft of the host was hiding in its midst. If he had actually been guilty, extradition would have been justified. The dilemma resulted from the fact that he was probably innocent but that his accusers would condemn him regardless.[2] What was to be done seeing that if the fanaticized hunters did not get him they would wreak their wrath on all the rest?

Naturally, in the course of two thousand years, differently placed sectors of Jewry have dealt with the problem in different ways. During the Crusades there was indeed an occasional weakening of community discipline and pride.[3] On the whole, however, a rather firm attitude has been kept up throughout the ages.

One difficulty in all this is to determine when a regime can be called alien and oppressive as opposed to legitimate. In the state of Israel today, there is no death penalty. Even if there were, in general, a group would not risk extermination or even imprisonment in order to protect a murderer. Still, there is a sizeable dissentient band for whom the present rulers are a damnable lot, and in certain circumstances it would probably do a great deal to prevent them from laying hands on a member. I suppose there are equally alienated segments in the United States.

In the New Testament, in the Fourth Gospel,[4] the high priest, Caiaphas, is in favour of contriving Jesus's death because if he went on with his doings, the Romans might be fed up with such independence as Judaea still possessed and make an end of

---

[1] An edition and translation by Schochet is due to appear shortly.
[2] Nowadays still, the question of whether the courts of the state requesting extradition can be trusted to be tolerably fair plays a part.
[3] See Daube op. cit., pp. 80 ff.   [4] John 11.49 ff.

the Temple and people. 'They shall take away', it is feared, 'both our place and nation'. So he contends: 'It is better that one man should die for the people and that the whole nation perish not'. According to the rabbinical ruling of the time, we have seen that, whatever the risks or even the certainties, if you are confronted by a hostile tyranny, precisely the opposite principle operates: no yielding. The point is that for the Sadducees—and Caiaphas was a Sadducean high priest—the Roman government was legitimate, the recognized over-lord of the country. That his position was very controversial is indicated by the vehement tone in which he introduces it: 'You know nothing at all nor do you reflect. It is better that one man should die' etc. His target must have been the Pharisaic rabbis, those of zealot tendencies in particular. In relation to a proper god-fearing regime, they would have shared his view; and indeed, in a later period, we do find it expressed in almost identical phraseology, in defense of the compromise resolution which I outlined above and which does admit some title to law enforcement in the Romans. But at the time of the Johannine scene, the Pharisees were adamant in this matter and would not acknowledge the Roman rule as warranting the slightest concession. These heathens were usurpers, so, irrespective of consequences, you must not hand over to them or destroy for their sakes any member of the community.

The extradition of the Sicarii to the Romans in AD 73 offers a close parallel to Caiaphas's attitude. After Judaea was completely subdued, a number of implacable zealots made their way to Egypt, trying to stir up a revolt there. They nearly succeeded among the mass of the Jews, but the upper ranks managed to stave off the ruinous undertaking and to see that the dangerous men and their families were delivered up to the ruling power.[1] Their presence had been enough to cause Vespasian to have the Jewish temple of Onias at Leontopolis dismantled:[2] Caiaphas's fears were not empty.

6

Whatever may have been the conduct of Jesus and his disciples for most of the time, they cannot be included among groups exclusively dedicated to civil disobedience. For, on a decisive occasion, the leader, to the awed admiration of his followers,

---

[1] Josephus, *War* 7.10.1.409 ff.   [2] Josephus, *War* 7.10.2.420 ff.

resorted to violence. I am referring to the incident euphemisti-
cally called 'the Cleansing of the Temple' (the appellation is not
found in the Bible) which is reported in all four gospels.[1]

The Temple at Jerusalem was internationally famous. Its
clientele, by no means confined to Jews, came from all over the
world. Accordingly, in its forecourt, much business was trans-
acted: you would give foreign currency for native one, in particular—if you were a Jew—for the small coin payable as an
annual contribution; and you would purchase animals suitable
for sacrifice—oxen, cows, sheep, birds—as well as ritually clean
vessels.[2] It was the kind of scene characteristic of countless
ancient and modern sanctuaries. Jesus was infuriated by it. He
fell upon the participants in it, drove them out and overthrew
their furniture.

According to John, the event took place towards the beginning of the ministry. This is historically unacceptable. I am
aware of sporadic attempts to defend it.[3] But it is unthinkable
that such a movement should start violently, with the administration looking on and doing nothing; that it should then turn
peaceful; and that when this had gone on for a while, it should
be put down. The sequence preserved by the synoptic gospels
is the historically correct one. It was this transition to violence
—in the nature of a sedition, as we shall see[4]—which, coming
after some two years of non-violent agitation, precipitated the
catastrophic intervention of the authorities.

The degree to which pacifists, or even non-pacifists who dis-
like seeing Jesus involved in active violence, repudiate this
episode is remarkable. (Another one which, for different
reasons, is found almost equally uncomfortable is that of the
Gadarene swine.[5]) A few years ago, at Oxford, I discussed
Jesus's methods with a great historian, an agnostic if not an
atheist, with, however, as I found out later, a mother who had
been a missionary in foreign parts. Believe it or not, this scholar,
among whose specialities is the New Testament epoch, did not
remember the incident; more than that, when I described it to
him, he denied it as impossible. I then shewed him the texts.

---

[1] Matthew 21.12 ff., Mark 11.15 ff., Luke 19.45 f., John 2.14 ff.
[2] Cp. Zechariah 14.21: in Messianic times, as everything is clean, the
suppliers of these vessels will be dispensable. See below, p. 108, n. 1.
[3] See *e.g.* Stauffer, *Jesus, Gestalt und Geschichte*, 1957, pp. 18, 56 ff.
[4] Below pp. 103, 108 f.
[5] Matthew 8.28 ff., Mark 5.1 ff., Luke 8.26 ff. Not in John.

His immediate gut response was: 'Oh, then Jesus must have forgotten himself on that occasion'.

More recently, another friend, a leading New Testament theologian, told me that we must not label what Jesus here did as violent: it was merely a symbolic act, prophetic symbolism. Before looking at this escape route, a word on a yet different one, tempting maybe a few decades ago when it was fashionable to discover fabrications though at the moment the tendency is to believe the sources. The solution I have in mind is to throw doubt on the veracity of the account: this terrible thing never happened. I have, however, seen no argument in the least convincing. Details are, of course, negotiable.[1] But that some outbreak of the nature outlined in all the gospels did occur is certain. It would not have been made up from nothing. On the contrary, suppression by the preachers and transmitters of tradition would be far more likely in a case like this than invention. Luke, who addresses a largely gentile public, does make drastic use of his scissors. He omits, for example, the awkwardly unphilosophical overturning of chairs and tables.[2]

Let us now inspect the prevalent method of emasculating this assault: its classification as mere prophetic symbolism—yes, Jesus did proceed in the fashion described, but he meant no harm to the individuals before him, his real intention was to protest the profanation of the holy place and initiate a religion elevated, spiritual, high above mundane commerce, fit for a redeemed, united world. On the whole, I concur with this interpretation of his measure. In fact, I have myself drawn attention to the Old Testament chapter about King Hezekiah's ejection of impure objects from the Temple as a possible influence behind the New Testament story.[3] Only it in no way removes the violence from the latter. What the symbolism does in this situation is to turn the affair from a common crime into a political one. Jesus intervenes as if by an authority superior to the regular, earthly one.[4] It smacks of sedition. Yet none of this, I repeat, gets rid of the violence.

---

[1] For example Mark's and Luke's description, according to which only a modest number of the objectionable people were thrown out—'he began to drive out'—is more credible than Matthew's and John's total evacuation—'he drove out all'.

[2] See also below, p. 106.

[3] See Daube, *He that cometh*, 1966, pp. 2f.

[4] It is noteworthy that, in all four gospels, Jesus is challenged to pro-

There is practically no human act complete in itself; almost invariably an act signifies something beyond. Admittedly, there are variations. Some acts carry less symbolism than others and —this, too, is important—what symbolism there is may be on a rather unconscious level in one case, intentional in another.[1] The onslaught under discussion is (I agree with the apologists) symbolic in the highest degree and undertaken in full awareness of its design. But the violence remains. The students at Irvine who burned the Bank of America had no quarrel with this particular manager, they probably had their accounts elsewhere; they wanted to denounce a rotten system. When extreme racists lynched a black they had never set eyes on before, they were promulgating an idea. Conversely, one need not even read Eldridge Cleaver's illuminating *Soul on Ice* to understand that the rape of a white woman by a black—at night, at some obscure spot, he does not know her, does not see her, does not give a hoot for this girl—is laden with symbolism. Would you say that the firing of the Bank, the lynching, the rape, were therefore non-violent, civil disobedience? I do not accept it.

The holders of the view I am combating will reply that I am overlooking the distinction between ordinary symbolism and prophetic symbolism: the latter is of a special kind. Granted, but it has no magic that neutralizes violence.[2] There seems to prevail a circular reasoning: prophetic symbolism is peaceful, the Cleansing was prophetic symbolism, ergo it was peaceful. However, if we define prophetic symbolism as peaceful, the Cleansing does not fall under it. If prophetic symbolism may be either peaceful or violent, the Cleansing does fall under it—under the latter variety. Usually, commentators on the Cleansing adduce only peaceful instances

duce his credentials directly or soon after the Cleansing of the Temple. See Daube, *The New Testament and Rabbinic Judaism*, 1956, pp. 220 ff.

[1] Even where a symbolical act is planned, there may attach to the very planning a meaning hidden from the planner. No need to pursue this here.

[2] Prophetic symbolism is a great arena for romantic theories. What may be termed anticipatory realism, for example, has been grossly overworked. Certainly, for the believers, to some extent, a prophet's act— say, Samuel's tearing off a piece of Saul's mantle: 'The Lord hath rent the kingdom from thee' (I Samuel 15.27 f.)—is not mere prefigurement, is already the event. But the qualification 'to some extent' is a heavy one, too often lost sight of with the queerest results. For the present study, it is not necessary to expand.

of prophetic symbolism:[1] Isaiah walking naked and barefoot in anticipation of the defeat of Egypt and Ethiopia,[2] Jeremiah finding his loincloth perished just as God finds the Jews worthless[3]—the same prophet carried a yoke on his shoulders to indicate submission to Babylon[4]—Agabus binding his hands and feet with Paul's belt as a prediction of the latter's forthcoming arrest.[5] These prophets smashed neither person nor property in performing their symbolism. The parallels are unobjectionable so long as we bear in mind that Jesus's demonstration was not so tame. There is, of course, no lack of violent models. When Phinehas speared a Hebrew and the Midianite woman he had brought into the camp,[6] that was to a considerable extent symbolical. Elijah slaughtered four hundred and fifty priests of the heathen god Baal—for the purity of the cult of the one God.[7] Who but a scholar in an ivory tower could deny violence in these cases? You ask that couple or those priests or, for that matter, the men beaten up by Jesus, whether there was no difference between Isaiah going about without clothes on and physical suppression. In my lecture on Prophets,[8] I comment on their modes of disobedience; and one of my major points is precisely a cleavage between the earlier prophets who were violent, almost men of war, and the later ones who were civil, who refrained from violence. The fact, for better or worse, is that Jesus did not so refrain.

I say for better or worse: I am not so sure whether those who boggle at the narrative have fully thought through the role of violence and the problem whether somewhere there might be a place for it. Again, even within violence there are momentous gradations. I hold it greatly in favour of the present Greek regime that, whatever else they may have done, they have not murdered any of their opponents. It is clear that no fatalities resulted in the course of the Cleansing of the Temple. This is a vital dividing line; and it gives one food for reflection that, in our day, an offence like the burning down of the Bank of America, where no death ensued, evoked a far more passionate condemnation on the part of the academic authorities (not to

---

[1] Johnson, Matthew, in *The Interpreter's Bible*, 7, 1951, p. 504, quotes Isaiah 20, Jeremiah 13 and Acts 21.
[2] Isaiah 20.1 ff.   [3] Jeremiah 13.1 ff.   [4] Jeremiah 27.1 ff.
[5] Acts 21.11 f. Things did not turn out exactly as foretold.
[6] Numbers 25.6 ff.   [7] I Kings 18.40.
[8] See above, Prophets and Philosophers, p. 64.

mention those outside) than several incidents where one side or the other managed to kill.

Given the use of violence in this episode, then, what was it, it may be asked, that so provoked Jesus? Why violence here and not on any number of other occasions—say, in controversy with pettifogging or even trap-setting critics, or when arraigned before the Sanhedrin? Uneducated readers often assume that he was incensed by dishonest exploitation of the pilgrims. This motive rarely now figures in the academic commentaries. There is not the trace of a hint at it in the texts. Furthermore, in the earliest account, the Markan one, which is adopted by Matthew, the pilgrims themselves are set upon: 'he began to cast out those that sold and bought'. Luke cuts out the buyers—for his public this would be excessive—and John follows him. The same considerations, however, rule out also the usual line of modern exegetes: the higher Sadducean priests who owned animal markets were the cause of Jesus' wrath.[1] The story makes no mention of it, and it is inconsistent with the attack on the buyers. Worse: this explanation leaves the moneychangers in the air—the priestly nobility had nothing to do with them, and it totally neglects the notice in Mark that Jesus 'would not suffer that any man should carry any vessel through the temple'. This detail is dropped by all later evangelists: it concerns too technical an observance regarding the Temple. But surely, it is all the more valuable: no analysis that does not come to grips with it can lay claim to plausibility.

What enraged Jesus was the visible, tangible disturbance of the ideal, sacred atmosphere. The carrying of objects through the holy area instead of a longer route around it,[2] the trading and moneychanging introduced a dissonance as intolerable as that of which Jeremiah—whom Jesus quotes—had complained.[3] He had reproved murderers, adulterers, idolaters who facilely thought the Temple would save them; that was to treat it, he had pointed out, like a brigands' shelter. For Jesus, the crowds visiting without showing proper respect were just as bad.[4] No doubt many people committed far graver transgres-

---

[1] See Johnson, Matthew, in *The Interpreter's Bible*, **7**, 1951, p. 504, Rengstorf, *Das Evangelium nach Lukas*, 9th ed., 1962, p. 221.

[2] Cp. Mishnah Berakoth 9.5, against suchlike indifference.

[3] Jeremiah 7.11.

[4] This is a notable case where the Old Testament precedent is concerned with morally reprehensible sins while Jesus focuses on appearances.

sions. But here was conspicuous vulgarity. It is significant that his violence was directed against small folk: moneychangers, not bankers,[1] sellers of doves—doves were sacrificed by the poor,[2] and his own mother after his birth had brought this sacrifice.[3] It is not only that, as in all cultures, the bigwigs—bankers, wealthy merchants, landowners—were too strong and well-protected to be manhandled; or that they would have been less readily frightened and impressed by a display of authority than their inferiors. The main factor is that the paltry, pitiful, unmanicured bustle of the lower orders acutely offends certain sensitivities, clashes with the aspiration after the perfect, the spotless. His upsetting of the furniture accords with this: he was irritated beyond measure by the indecorous spectacle.[4]

John, as already remarked, transposes the incident to the opening of Jesus' public activity, thus bestowing on it a pro-grammatic character. Accordingly he depicts Jesus as a tower-ing figure executing judgment. Jesus personally makes a savage thong and he uses it to expel not only the traders and money-changers but also the oxen and sheep offered for sale—beasts not mentioned in the other gospels at all: an exercise of might. Even John, however, refers to the doves,[5] and Jesus, besides overturning the tables of the moneychangers, pours out their coins.[6] Moreover, instead of quoting Jeremiah's remonstrance

---

[1] Klostermann, *Das Markus-Evangelium*, 4th ed., 1950, p. 117, is wrong when he writes: *kollybistes = trapezites*. The former transacts petty business, the latter has an established firm. Matthew 25.27 does speak of bankers: the slothful servant ought to have invested his master's money with them. Heine, alluding to the Cleansing, apostrophizes Jesus (*Deutschland*, ch. 13; see Elster, *Heines sämtliche Werke*, 2, p. 457): *Geldwechsler, Bankiers has du sogar Mit der Peitsche gejagt aus dem Tempel*. The poet is of course entitled to insert the unhistorical bankers in order to extend the condemnation to that fraternity—and indeed to a particular member of it, his uncle Salomon Heine.

[2] Leviticus 5.7, 12.8, 14.22, 15.14, 29.   [3] Luke 2.24.

[4] Psychoanalytical findings come to mind, but I shall leave them alone.

[5] Naturally, they cannot be driven out with a lash, like the oxen and sheep: Jesus, John informs us, orders their vendors to take them away. This order—with the implication that it is obeyed—also belongs to the element of might stressed by John.

[6] Interestingly, one cannot pour out banknotes or cheques. One can tear them up, but that is a different matter. For one thing, it is slower. McCabe, in *San Francisco Chronicle* of 19 January 1972, p. 37, tells of 'a fellow named Mike who married a lady because she took up one of his $50 bills from a restaurant table and calmly tore it to bits'. It does

against the Temple's degradation into a brigands' cave, he is represented as directly objecting to its use as a bazaar.[1]

As a Californian I would add a further reflection. Our kids would react very negatively to an overemphasis on the symbolical component. 'What?', they would say, 'he was not really angry with the mob he threw out? That is shocking. We understand all sorts of emotions, and to hit somebody whom you passionately hate at that moment is not unforgivable. Some people deserve to be hit. But to hit somebody you are not personally cross with, in order to make an ideological point, that is to use him as a tool. It goes on constantly in our society, in many different ways, and it is one of the mean, dishonest, dehumanizing things we most object to'.

It would be interesting to find out at what moment, at what place and in what milieu it was first felt desirable to tone down or eliminate the violence of the Cleansing, even more interesting to trace the fortunes of this undertaking. The inquiry would, of course, reach right into the present,[2] and future historians could continue it. It would throw much light on basic and often submerged presuppositions of New Testament researchers, including myself.

We might speculate what the governmental response to an action of this nature would be in our time. The Jewish leaders

---

not follow that he would have married her if she had spilled coins of his to the same amount.

[1] Cp. Zechariah 14.21, cited above, p. 102, n. 2.

[2] This may be the place to observe that even among believing Christian scholars there are those who accept the account as it stands. Gossip, John, in *The Interpreter's Bible*, 8, 1952, pp. 497f., expounds: 'Desperate attempts have been made by some who feel uncomfortable over it to tone down and edge out the incident . . . But . . . this was a wild scene, with cowering figures clutching desperately at their tables, as these were flung here and there; or running after their spilled coins, as these rolled hither and thither; or shrinking from the lash that had no mercy till the holy place was cleansed . . . If this incident had been recorded of anyone else in history, it would universally have been accepted as the scene of violence it was. And those who try to explain it away do so because they feel unhappily that it will not fit into their preconceived ideas of what Christ should do and be; that here somehow he acted for once out of character, and fell inexplicably below himself, forgot his own law of life, lost his head and temper . . . And the best thing to do is to say as little about it as one can . . . But that is foolishness.' Gossip heads this section (p. 496): 'The Danger of Caricaturing Christ'.

then at the helm, perpetually looking over their shoulders as to whether their Roman chiefs might be alarmed and step in, concluded that they had better subdue this group.[1]

A glance at two other sections of the gospels—the Sermon on the Mount and Jesus's arrest—may round off this discussion.

In the Sermon on the Mount, Jesus is represented as proclaiming: 'You have heard, An eye for an eye and a tooth for a tooth, but I say unto you, That you resist not evil, but whosoever shall smite thee on thy right cheek turn to him the other also.'[2] This is frequently adduced in favour of a pacifist attitude. Historically, however, that is not its import at all. In the current interpretation of the time, the biblical provision 'an eye' and so forth[3] meant that he who is guilty of a deliberate physical assault must pay not only for any damage and for medical expenses but also for the contempt involved.[4] It is chiefly the meek acceptance of scorn which Jesus is here advocating—or portrayed as advocating: I am not concerned in this context with the authenticity of the teaching. A slap in the face is the standard example of an insulting attack in ancient legal or moral exposition.[5] That is why he concentrates on this case. If he had intended to exclude violent retaliation in general, he could not have given so mild an instance. We today can put it to wider use and generalize it so as to cover the most serious situations: when your country is invaded do not shoot; when an armed burglar comes to your house do not ward him off; when a gangster threatens you or your family with a revolver, do not oppose him with force, and if he has killed your child, exact no retribution. We can do this, but we are thereby enormously

---

[1] As these lectures go to the Press, an essay by Raymond Lloyd reaches me entitled Cross and Psychosis, Creativeness and Envy (reprinted from *Faith and Freedom*, **24**, parts 1, 1970, and **2**, 1971). The Cleansing is here interpreted (pp. 18f., 25) as a phase of a breakdown of Jesus ultimately brought about by the envy of his opponents: but for his crucifixion, this psychosis, being a healing process, might well have been followed by a stressless exploitation of his great gifts. The argument is profound and moving. Nonetheless, it, too, betrays a reluctance to identify the ideal Jesus with this scene; and this remains true even should the thesis be correct.

[2] Matthew 5.38f. See Daube, *The New Testament and Rabbinic Judaism*, 1956, pp. 254ff.

[3] Exodus 21.24.   [4] Mishnah Baba Qamma 8.1.

[5] E.g. Isaiah 50.6, Matthew 26.67f., Mark 14.65, Luke 22.64, John 18.22, Mishnah Baba Qamma 8.6, Gellius 20.1.13.

expanding the sense. Originally what was counselled was to submit to humiliating treatment humbly and put your aggressor to shame by turning the other cheek.

It is relevant that Jesus quotes only 'an eye for an eye, a tooth for a tooth', omitting the first member of the old formula: 'a life for a life'.[1] The reason is that murder then was in principle still subject to capital punishment, however carefully checked. He does not contest this part of the retaliatory slogan. He confines himself to that which, in that period, was taken to ordain compensation for insulting attacks: according to him they should be put up with in patience. His exhortation really corresponds to the rabbinic prayer: 'And to those that curse me let my soul be dumb; yea, let my soul be like dust unto all'.[2] This Matthean saying, then, cannot be employed to show that he condemned violence as such.

According to the gospel of Mark,[3] when those sent to arrest Jesus had taken hold of him, one of his disciples cut off with his sword an ear of the high priest's servant who was among the detachment. It is important to note that this is not an attempt to prevent the arrest. Jesus, at this moment, is already in the hands of his pursuers. The action constitutes an expression of scorn, a forceful insult. Contemporary sources report several cases of one person slitting or lopping off another's ear as an extreme gesture of contempt. If a priest suffers this mutilation, he becomes indeed unfit for ritual service.[4] Jesus's disciple could not get at the high priest himself but at least, by such ill-use of his servant, he was showing what he thought of the master. There are many cases in ancient literature, including the Bible,[5] where you put down the master through his servant. It is, then, a case of insult, not resistance. Moreover, in this earliest Markan account of the scene, Jesus does not reprimand his disciple in the very least. On the contrary, he reproaches those who have seized him for their cowardly and devious conduct.

Let us go on to Matthew.[6] The action of the temperamental disciple still follows the capture of Jesus. But by now, it is seen

---

[1] Exodus 21.23.

[2] *Authorised Daily Prayer Book*, transl. Singer, 9th ed., 1912, p. 54.

[3] Mark 14.47. See Daube, *Journal of Theological Studies*, new series, 11, 1960, pp. 59ff.

[4] Tosephta Parah 3.8, Josephus, *Jewish Antiquities* 14.13.10.366, *Jewish War* 1.13.10.270.

[5] II Samuel 10.4f., I Chronicles 19.4f.   [6] Matthew 26.51ff.

as an attempt to free him and he does protest: 'Put up thy sword'. Indeed, he utters a stern warning: 'All they that take the sword shall perish with the sword.'

Then comes an interesting addition. Jesus says that if he wished to escape he could easily do so: he could command ever so many angels to release him. He does not summon them because he recognizes the necessity that the scriptural predictions concerning his suffering be fulfilled. This raises a problematic aspect of saints in this situation. If you know that you could overwhelm your opponent, that in fact you have supernatural power, it puts you into a state entirely different from that of a weak, defenseless man. However, I shall not dwell on this complication.

Between Mark and Matthew, then, the assault has turned from insult into resistance, into an effort to undo the arrest, and Jesus disapproves. Here we are on the way to some degree at least of pacifism. Exactly how radical it is depends on the meaning of the quotation 'All they that take the sword' etc. On the face of it, it is very comprehensive, as is a comparable maxim in Revelation.[1]

In Luke[2] a further stage has been reached: the assault now occurs as Jesus is threatened with arrest, that is to say, before they have actually laid hands on him. This switch is very much emphasized: at the approach of Judas, the disciples ask Jesus whether they should draw their swords, and that the question precedes the arrest is made doubly clear by a reference to their motivation—'they saw the *esomenon*',[3] 'what was about to happen', 'what would come about'.

Before Jesus can answer, one of his disciples cuts off the right ear of the high priest's servant. (It has become the right ear.) Jesus goes as far as to heal that ear, yet makes only a brief remark: 'Let it be thus far'. There is no saying in general rejection of force. As far as the treatment of the enemy is concerned, we have moved further towards a kindly attitude; as for verbal teaching, the basic point is not raised at all.

John[4] sides with Luke in that the action takes place before Jesus is in fact apprehended. Peter cuts off an ear of the high priest's servant. Jesus tells him to put up his sword: he is resigned to drink the cup of suffering. There is no stress here on

---

[1] Revelation 13.10.   [2] Luke 22.49ff.   [3] Future participle of 'to be'.
[4] John 18.10f.

any wrong of violence. Peter is to desist simply because Jesus must go through with what God has allotted to him.

In sum, the earliest gospel, Mark, presumably nearest to the events, knows of no disapproval on the part of Jesus at all. One of the disciples with fiercely insulting intent cuts off an ear of the high priest's servant and that is that. It happens after the arrest. Gradually the original significance of the attack is forgotten; by the time of Luke, it is definitely undertaken to ward off the arrest, it is transposed to the moment the pursuers arrive. The movement towards condemnation of resistance is rather chequered. Matthew alone has an apparently pacifist motto. Luke, while noting that Jesus heals the person injured (perhaps particularly important in the eyes of this evangelist—a physician), contains no express objection to violence. Nor does John. Jesus stops his defender because the time for submission has come; and he is not, as in Luke, represented as healing the maimed servant. Conceivably John favours a less irenic attitude than Matthew and Luke. It will be recalled[1] that his version of the Cleansing of the Temple is distinctly more gruesome than any of the other three.

7

The narrative of Peter's denial as well as some later apostolic experiences illumine details of the rabbinic teaching in the matter of civil resistance.

As stated above,[2] idolatry is to be shunned even if your life depends on it; and disavowal of one's Jewishness counts as pretty close to idolatry. The rabbis, in dealing with the problem of disavowal under duress, make two basic distinctions: first, between evasion and a straight No, and second, between private and public action. An unreserved 'I am not a Jew' is worse than ambiguous phrasing or dissimulation by conduct, and to cave in in front of a gathering worse than when coerced by just one or two bandits. As for the former distinction, the ancient commentators on the Book of Esther are at pains to explain that even before she revealed her antecedents, she never lied about them, merely kept silent or equivocated.[3] Again,

---

[1] See above, pp. 108f. [2] See pp. 97f.
[3] Targum Sheni 8.7. The original indeed represents Esther merely as withholding information, not as giving false one: 'Esther had not showed her people', Esther 2.10, 20.

during a persecution around AD 100 certain young scholars dressed like gentiles: all right so long as they would not repudiate their religion in so many words.[1] The latter distinction, between private and public, runs throughout law and morality. Steadfastness demonstrated strengthens the communal spirit, it impresses outsiders, it is that great thing the rabbis call 'sanctification of the name'. Daniel, Mordecai, the Maccabean martyrs are models. So important is the impact of the public gesture that, in the view of one school, during a period of persecution your practice must be more, not less, stringent than usual, you must not even transgress the slightest commandment in order to save your life.[2] Conversely, lapse in public weakens the fibre of the community and damages its standing in the outside world; it is 'profanation of the name'. When Moses struck the rock, the rabbis tell us, it was the public exhibition of disbelief which merited the terrible punishment of exclusion from the promised land.[3] Private wrong-doing is far less critical: according to some rabbis, if you will otherwise be killed, you may even commit idolatry provided it is not public.[4] The New Testament is thoroughly familiar with this thinking: 'Whosoever shall confess me before men, him I will confess also before my Father which is in heaven, but whosoever shall deny me before men, him will I also deny before my Father which is in heaven'.[5]

To come to Peter's denial,[6] the Markan account[7] offers a perfect illustration of the rabbinic principles. Jesus has been arrested and is undergoing a painful interrogation in the high priest's palace. In the courtyard, Peter is warming himself by a fire. Earlier in that night, when he had assured Jesus that he would in no circumstances desert him, Jesus had predicted: 'Before the cock crows twice, thou shalt deny me thrice'. Now a maid of the high priest's recognizes him: 'And thou also wast with Jesus of Nazareth'. To which he retorts: 'I neither know nor understand what thou sayest'. This, his first denial, takes place in private, to one person, and it is an evasion, he pre-

---

[1] Genesis Rabba 82 on 35.17.
[2] Tosephta Shabbath 16.17, Babylonian Sanhedrin 74 a.
[3] Tanhuma on Numbers 20.12.
[4] Babylonian Sanhedrin 74 a, Abodah Zarah 27 b, Siphra on Leviticus 18.5.
[5] Matthew 10.32 f., Luke 12.8 f.; cp. Mark 8.38, Luke 9.26.
[6] See Daube, *Theology* 72, 1969, pp. 291 ff.   [7] Mark 14.66 ff.

tends not to get her meaning. He now steps into the porch in order to shake her off, but she follows him 'and began to say to them that stood by, This is one of them'. He gives the same answer as before. So he still makes an evasive statement, as if he did not comprehend, but this time in public. The story goes on: 'And a little after, they that stood by said again to Peter, Surely thou art one of them, for thou art a Galilean and thy speech agreeth thereto. But he began to curse and to swear, I know not this man of whom ye speak. And the second time the cock crew'. This third denial, in direst straits, is both public and decided.

Matthew's version of the three denials[1] corresponds less closely to the rabbinic categories. All three are in public, the first evasive, the second and third direct. Luke[2] manifestly does not appreciate them at all. But doctor and subtle psychologist that he is, he prefers a different sequel. All three denials take place in public. It is the first two which are direct, 'I know him not' and 'I am not one of them', and the last which takes the form 'I know not what thou sayest'. Ordinarily, if you are accused of belonging to a seditious band, to play dumb, to maintain that you have not even heard of it, that you do not even follow the charge, is a more extreme dissociation than just to affirm that you do not know the leader or that you are not a member. It is in this sense, as a climax, that Luke places at the end 'I do not know what thou sayest'—since he is unaware of the technical reason this answer comes first in the earlier tradition, namely, as a prevarication in contrast to an outright repudiation. John,[3] like Matthew and Luke, has all three denials in public; and he introduces even more uniformity by having them all direct.

Whether Peter in reality proceeded exactly as Mark has it, who can say? What one can say, however, is that the two distinctions governing his behaviour have their roots so deep in human nature that they would be well within the grasp of the simpler people. Circumlocution versus directness and conduct behind closed doors versus conduct in the public eye: there is no stratum of society where these pairs of opposites are not greatly in evidence.

---

[1] Matthew 26.69ff.   [2] Luke 22.55ff.

[3] John 18.16ff. This evangelist's treatment must be seen in conjunction with the scene where the risen Jesus asks Peter three times whether he loves him and Peter three times gives practically the same reply: 'Thou knowest that I love thee'; John 21.15ff.

Later on,[1] when Peter and his fellow-apostles preached the risen Jesus at Jerusalem, the Sanhedrin was particularly incensed since it was dominated by Sadducees, who rejected bodily resurrection. The apostles, however, courageously spurned all warnings to desist. They declared they would obey God rather than men—language we met in earlier cases: the Hebrew midwives in Eygpt, the Mesopotamian soothsayer Balaam, Socrates.[2]

The Sanhedrin now contemplated killing them and placed them under arrest. But its most respected Pharisaic member, Gamaliel the Elder, Paul's master,[3] adduced examples of pseudo-Saviours who, without any effort on the Sanhedrin's part, after some initial success, had perished, and their cause with them. He concluded: 'Refrain from these men and let them alone; for if this counsel or work be of man, it will be overthrown, but if it be of God, ye cannot overthrow it, lest haply ye be found even to fight against God'. This plea introduces into the handling of heresy an element singularly Jewish, in fact, peculiar to an epoch marked by Messianic expectations. The advent of the Messiah may be heralded by happenings the nature of which is not yet fully manifest. Hence there is a degree of uncertainty regarding the Christian sect. Gamaliel's advice does not mean that, once a movement is definitely proved apostate, harsh suppression would not be in order.[4] Nor that one need remain totally passive in the face of what looks a serious challenge: the Sanhedrin, impressed by his argument, set the apostles free, but not without first having them flogged, and it is quite conceivable that he agreed to this procedure. What it does mean is that one should avoid irreversible steps, above all, bloodshed.

The rabbi is admirably explicit on the general justification of his approach, the basic assumptions rendering it the reasonable solution. Things may not immediately be recognizable for what they are. But on the one hand, if truly evil, God will not allow them to last; that is why you can afford to wait. On the

---

[1] Acts 4.1ff. See Daube, *California Law Review*, **59**, 1971, pp. 789ff.
[2] See above, The Women of the Bible and Greece, p. 5, Prophets and Philosophers, pp. 66, 76.
[3] Acts 22.3.
[4] It was when his grandson Gamaliel II was President of the Academy of Jabneh that an imprecation against Christians and other heretics became part of the daily Eighteen Benedictions.

other, if what appears suspect should really be salvation, sent in this testing guise, its triumph is assured and severity against it would be futile, indeed impious. As the Mishnah has it:'Any dispute that is in the name of Heaven shall end by standing up, but any not in the name of Heaven shall not'.[1] In one form or another, this trust is dominant in Judaism, Christianity and even beyond: think of the slogans 'history is on our side' and 'we shall overcome some day'. Without it, most long-term communal enterprises would make little sense. How to strike a balance between it and the urge to lend a helping hand to the deity's ideas (which happily, always coincide with one's own) is a notoriously difficult, perennial problem of theology.

Gamaliel's disciple Paul, inveighing against Jewish opponents of the Christian claim, deems it an extenuating circumstance that, however wrong-headed, they are prompted by genuine 'zeal of God'.[2] A conscientious straying is recognized as a lesser disgrace: at least it is not frivolous, it springs from a fundamentally devout disposition. The Talmud[3] distinguishes between two motives for setting aside the laws forbidding the eating of carrion: a man may set them aside from lust or he may do so in a spirit of defiance. While there is unanimity as to the former's untrustworthiness as a legal witness, one opinion would admit the latter. His crime is incomparably more terrible, yet precisely what makes it more terrible also proves his superior uprightness and consistency.

8

The very first Greek trial for *aseby*, impiety, crime against religion, of which we have any knowledge, was of Aeschylus.[4] He was charged with divulging—apparently in a play—one of the mysteries of the goddess Demeter. His defence was he had been unaware that the particular matter was a secret. Aristotle[5] refers to the episode among the types of ignorance; it falls under the case where you are ignorant of precisely what you are doing.

---

[1] Mishnah Aboth 5.17.
[2] Romans 10.1 f.; see Daube, *Sin, Ignorance and Forgiveness in the Bible*, 1960, pp. 28 ff.
[3] Babylonian Sanhedrin 27 a; see Petuchowski, *Hebrew Union College Annual*, **30**, 1959, pp. 179 ff.
[4] Lipsius, *Das Attische Recht und Rechtsverfahren*, **2**, pt. 1, 1908, p. 361.
[5] *Nichomachean Ethics* 3.1.17.111 a.

I am inclined to believe Aeschylus. He was highly traditional and would not, I think, defiantly have published a cult mystery. At any rate the court believed him: he was acquitted. By that time, an error of this kind—i.e. an assumption which, were it correct, would remove the act from the area of crime—was accepted as a good enough excuse.[1] We saw in the previous Lecture[2] that Socrates went a good deal further in admitting a plea of ignorance. The incident, despite its happy ending, illustrates the solicitousness of the priestly class for the preservation of their professional intimacies.[3]

The charge of *aseby* was ill-defined. The availability of the procedure as well as that of *eisaggely* should give one pause when one praises the freedom of Athens, even if one confines one's considerations to the citizens and discounts the slaves.

The trial by *eisaggely* could for centuries be held on the ground of almost any act regarded as a serious infringement of civic duty. It took place before the popular assembly; or at least it started there, for the assembly could delegate much of it to some court. The wide scope meant that, if a statesman fell from power, he was easily exposed to this trial with its risk of capital punishment. It could be directed against religiously suspect citizens as well as against such as were hateful on more narrowly political grounds.

I am not in these lectures dealing with political minorities. My main reason is that this would necessitate an intensive study of treason, a formidable subject I wish to avoid as far as possible. However, I feel I just cannot skip two items: one, the oldest surviving comedy in world literature, *The Acharnians* by Aristophanes, written and performed in the middle of a desperate, nonsensical war (much like the *Lysistrata*) and dealing with a problem which is as acute today as it was then; and two, a scandal at Rome concerning secret documents.

The hero of Aristophanes' play is fed up with the war which really helps only a small clique of generals and political profiteers. He decides to conclude a private peace treaty with the enemy for himself, his wife and his children. He is offered three samples, a treaty for five years, one for ten and one for thirty, and he chooses the thirty-years one. Now the fat is in the fire: while all the rest continue suffering, he trades with anybody,

---

[1] As for Jewish law, see e.g. Acts 23.3 ff.
[2] Above, Prophets and Philosophers, pp. 74 f. [3] Cp. below, pp. 120 f.

receives hospitably whoever comes along and has a good time. His compatriots, enraged at his doings, at first refuse even to give him a hearing. But he seizes as a hostage the sacred symbol of their economy, a scuttle—they were coal-burners—holds it up and threatens to destroy it if they hurt him. It is as if in the the United States one were to hold up a share in an oil company and to say: 'If you will not let me speak, I shall burn this'. So they listened to him and he troubles their minds greatly by stating what, deep-down, of course, they all know: that the enemy is not the only guilty party, that they themselves had acted in a reprehensible manner on several occasions, and that in any case to go on with this war is madness and brutality.

The comedy contrasts the well-thinking, stupid, simple citizen who follows the call to arms with the hero who has opted out. In the end the obedient citizen is brought onto the stage, returned from the war a cripple for life, while the disobedient one makes merry and enjoys himself. The former is helpless on a stretcher, the latter is surrounded by women and about to have a good dinner and a good night. The returned soldier laments: 'Oh, lift me gently round the hips, my comrades true.' The independent peace-maker exclaims: 'Oh, kiss me warmly on the lips, my darlings, do.' The returned soldier: 'My brain is dizzy with the blow of hostile stone.' The peacemaker: 'Mine's dizzy too. To bed I'll go and not alone.'[1] In this play the ordinary down-to-earth arguments and feeling against war and for peace are displayed.

By the way, the comedy was staged at a festival to which foreigners were not admitted. Aristophanes, through his actors, several times emphasizes their absence because an earlier play (not extant) in which he had made fun of the government had very nearly involved him—or his producer—in an unpleasant trial for defaming the state in the presence of aliens.[2] That was

---

[1] *The Acharnians* 1214ff. Translation by Rogers, *Aristophanes* (*Loeb Classical Library*), I, 1903, p. 117.

[2] Lipsius (op. cit., 1905, p. 200) holds that Cleon's charge after the performance of *The Babylonians* must have been preferred not against the poet but against Callistratus, who in that year was the man entrusted with the presentation of the festival plays. This theory is based on the consideration that the charge seems to have taken the form of *eisaggely*, generally confined to crimes by officers of state. Callistratus, directing part of the festival, might count as an officer; the poet would not. I am not fully convinced; the matter is very doubtful. The relevant passages in *The Acharnians* are 377, 503ff., 628ff., 659ff.

one of the charges that could be brought at the time against a vociferously critical citizen: these things do not change greatly in two or three thousand years.

Quite likely the fact that, on the whole, Aristophanes was a conservative made possible feats which avowed progressives could not have got away with. It does speak for the artistic and political courage of some people at the time at least, that the comedy was awarded first prize in a competition in the midst of war.

As for political minorities at Rome, the one episode I feel called on to mention in view of a recent happening in this country, is the illicit appropriation and publication of secret papers of the pontiffs around 300 B C. Up to that time the devices you had to use to be successful in litigation were jealously guarded in the archives of this body, consisting entirely of high aristocrats. So the ordinary fellow entering upon a suit was pretty much at their mercy. About 300, one of the most influential patricians of Rome was Appius Claudius. Though basically tied to the tradition of his class, he displayed great independence in his actions, caring little for criticism either from his peers or from below; he was an individuality. An accomplished jurist, he put together the procedural formulas used by the pontiffs. No doubt he knew them from experience as well as from his easy association with the informed circles. He did not go as far as to bring out his book himself, but he allowed his scribe, Cnaeus Flavius, son of one of his freedmen, to steal and publish it as well as the pontifical calendar of dates suitable or unsuitable for litigation and a number of other important transactions: that calendar had been one more means by which the pontiffs directed affairs the way they wanted. There was a terrific uproar, but Flavius got away with it—the first treason of a clerk. In fact, he became so popular with the common people that he attained office unusually high for one of his origin; mind you, by common people in this context we have to understand the well-to-do majority of heads-of-houses at Rome, common only by contrast with the exalted nobility. He was the latter's *bête noire*, of course, but he successfully countered all attempts to demolish him.[1]

Many details of the story have been questioned, and some

---

[1] Livy 9.46, 7, 9, 12, Valerius Maximus 2.5.2, 9.3.3, Pliny, *Natural History* 33.6.18 f.; see Münzer, Pauly-Wissowa, **6**, 1909, p. 2527.

hypercritical scholars reject it in its entirety. Wherever one may stand on this, we are here afforded a glimpse into Roman thinking about this kind of venture: good enough for this discussion.

I would not unreservedly subscribe to the maxim that knowledge is power; it can be paralysis. Still, the illicit divulging of secret material in a higher cause is invariably calculated to abridge the owner's discretion. Within this general aim, the action may be geared towards the most diverse particular results. You may wish to expose him as unfit for the office he is seeking; or to call attention to subversive influences. We are all familiar with the case where it is hoped to force the hand of a set by betraying its doings and plans to the critics at home and abroad. Flavius represents yet another type. His was a less narrow goal, he was out to achieve a rather fundamental reform. A professional body exercised control over outsiders, strictly excluded from access to its listed modes of operation. The revelation of these relieved the bondage.

Throughout history, the three occupations most reliant for their pre-eminence on secrecy of know-how are the priests, the lawyers and the medicals—taking these terms in the widest sense. We call them the professions; which is ironical seeing that they profess least. The housewives with inherited unique culinary recipes might be added as a fourth such order; and in modern times, certain industries sitting on exclusive techniques assume a similar character. A fuller investigation would indeed have to embrace those groups which, though not officially recognized, are purposefully united behind the scenes. Of course, it makes little difference whether the secrets are in written or unwritten form. To this day, unwritten ones are often of special importance: their transmission is necessarily from person to person, thus aiding the closeness of the circle.

It is not accidental that the professions whose rule is based on the possession of secrets at one time were more or less one. You had the priest-jurists—the pontiffs of Flavius's period, for example—and you had the priest-medics.[1] Their separation is by no means complete even now. The degree to which their

---

[1] A legislative form in the Bible going back to them is discussed by Daube, *Proceedings of Oxford Society of Historical Theology*, 1944–5, pp. 39 ff., and Yaron, *Introduction to the Law of the Aramaic Papyri*, 1961, pp. 110 ff.

work is withdrawn from vulgar gaze is quite remarkable. In many countries, say, conveyancing, the transfer of land, indeed most branches of the law, could be immensely simplified. But these intricate requirements and little provisos which no average sane person comprehends or would even desire to comprehend secure the professional's reign. That is why, a moment ago, I said that Flavius's act of civil disobedience 'relieved' the bondage. It did not terminate it: the pontiffs had at their disposal more than one method of keeping the judicial area opaque. An aunt of mine was famous in the family for her absolutely inimitable cheesecake, and she never lost her status. If the Pentagon papers had been guarded half as well as her recipe, Dr Ellsberg would have got nowhere.

It would be foolish to contend that secrecy has no place in public life. (As for private life, it is so essential as to admit only of the tiniest inroads.[1]) No leadership and no following could afford revealing all its deliberations and actions: the former would tumble in no time, the latter would stand no chance of ever improving its lot. The professions have good, additional grounds for reticence: one of them being that the very efficacy of a religious, legal or medical procedure in large measure depends on the party's surrender to something that passes his understanding. (This holds good also for much that goes on in private relations. The veil has its uses. Magic imports meaning.) Nevertheless people will always feel that there comes a point where concentration of expertise in the hands of a few entails exploitation and oppression of the many; and now and then the resentment may be strong enough to make illicit rectification appear a right, if not a duty. Exactly when such matters come to a head varies hugely in different epochs and cultures—not to forget the role of outstanding persons at a decisive moment.

The collaboration with the robber of an insider—or near-insider—like Flavius's master is a frequent phenomenon. 'We are betrayed by what is false within'. The Sybilline Oracles, consulted whenever Rome was in an extreme crisis, were originally entrusted to two prominent citizens appointed by the

---

[1] It may well become possible so to listen in to another person's brain-waves as to read his thoughts without any communication on his part; perhaps one will be able to tap even one's own waves. The human species will then quickly disappear.

king. It was one of the two very first guardians who gave away information from the collection. He was less lucky than Flavius. Instead of being rewarded, he was sewed up in a leather bag—probably together with a dog, a cock, a viper and an ape—and thrown into the sea.[1] (I bet even the new Supreme Court would tend to regard this as cruel and unusual punishment.) The matter did not, however, rest there. In course of time, the plebeians found that the Oracles had a way of containing matter favourable to the patricians from whom the custodians continued to be selected. They finally, in 367 BC, got a fresh board constituted, half patricians and half plebeians.[2]

In this area no less than in others, violent self-help supplements civil. Instead of citing examples, let me remind you of the familiar tales of sorcerers forced by brave heroes to part with their spell: the essential thrust is the same as in the case of Flavius. As school children, we are invited to admire the victors in these combats, and even their successors in historical narrative. Later on, our betters prefer us less enthusiastic.

---

[1] Dionysius of Halicarnassus 4.62.4. The translation 'and when one of those men seemed to have been faithless'—Cary, on the basis of Spelman, *Dionysius of Halicarnassus* (*Loeb Classical Library*), 2, 1939, p. 467—is literal but misleading. Behind the 'seemed' stands Latin *videri* referring to a verdict: 'he was found to have been faithless', found guilty of it. See Daube, *Forms of Roman Legislation*, 1956, pp. 73 ff. Why the man's punishment was that of a parricide is a puzzle; see Mommsen, *Römisches Strafrecht*, 1899, pp. 567 f., 921 ff.

[2] Livy 6.37.12, 6.42.2.

ASPIRANTS TO STATEHOOD

A breakaway movement within a state (the radical wing of the Scottish Nationalists) or within an empire (the freedom fighters in British Honduras) may employ peaceful or violent methods; and in the former case, it may work within the law—by means of petitions and negotiations—or make use also of illicit devices, civil disobedience—wildcat strikes, sit-ins in public buildings, refusal to pay taxes. There are regimes where the mere expression of a wish for separation constitutes high treason, so that no legal route is conceivable and the choice lies between peaceful and violent illegality.

History, it appears, knows no successful independence movement which kept strictly within the law,[1] and very few which refrained from violence. Let me remind you that I include in violence a dire threat even if it does not materialize. Suppose a colony kidnaps and holds hostage the governor and his family and makes ready to receive any police from the mother-country with heavy artillery, that is not civil disobedience. On the other hand, where the general picture is pacific, an occasional erratic act of violence would not, for the purpose of this discussion, alter it. However, as just remarked, the instances of civil disobedience sufficing to accomplish a breakaway are exceedingly rare. India, which may spring to mind, is definitely not one of them. The impressive figure of Gandhi tends to make us forget about the continuous bloodshed accompanying that nation's progress; to further this forgetfulness has so far suited both British and Indian mythographers—if for different reasons. Quite recently, Southern Rhodesia became a Republic peacefully: there was neither an actual clash with Britain nor the

---

[1] Altbaden, where I was born and grew up, fought by legal means and lost. New York City's struggle is in an early phase; see *San Francisco Chronicle* of June 9, 1971. *Passport to Pimlico* is fondly remembered.

remotest likelihood of one. Another modern example is Norway's split from Sweden, effected, as a law professor commented at the time, 'with a truly disconcerting simplicity and tenacity.'[1] The 14th International Peace Congress happened to be in session at the Hague and congratulated Norway 'on obtaining complete independence without the shedding of a drop of blood,' and Sweden 'on the noble self-denial in recognizing Norway's unanimous desire for an amicable separation.'[2] Still, how exceptional such friendly partings are may be gauged from the fact that, in text-books on international law, when we look up the Index under Secession, we are apt to be referred to Revolt—a distinctly more belligerent term.[3]

I propose to say a few words on two Old Testament cases, the exodus from Egypt and the foundation of the Northern Kingdom, and then to analyze in some detail the abortive plebeian secessions at Rome.

1

The exodus story depicts the Hebrews as a grievously oppressed people in an alien land. They are concentrated in a certain geographical area,[4] but as the men at least are forced to work as slaves on buildings and estates, there must be some dispersal. Like many a race in a similar condition,[5] they form a majority compared with their masters; and the latter are worried lest in the event of an attack from outside, they might join up with the enemy and depart.[6] From time immemorial, the involvement of a country in a war has provided opportunities, on the one hand for the governing set, if those held down fear the foreign peril most of all and will therefore rally round their superiors,[7] and on the other hand for those held down, if they are ambivalent or definitely judge the present government the worst con-

---

[1] Cornil, *Revue de Droit International*, 38, 1906, p. 222.

[2] I quote from the *Chronicle des Faits Internationaux*, in *Revue Générale de Droit International Public*, 12, 1905, p. 655.

[3] *E.g.*, Oppenheim, *International Law*, 1, 8th ed. by Lauterpacht, 1955, p. 1063.

[4] Exodus 8.18, 9.26.

[5] The black population of South Africa far outnumbers its rulers.

[6] Exodus 1.9 f.

[7] 'Most experts attribute the emergence of Israel's Black Panthers to . . . the Mideast cease-fire, which has diverted public attention from border bloodshed to internal matters': Eliason in *San Francisco Chronicle* of May 16, 1971, p. 27.

ceivable and will therefore exploit its predicament. We shall find the phenomenon illustrated both by the defection of the Northern tribes and by the Roman development.[1]

Two fables come to mind. One[2] preaches contentedness with a regime however loathsome since what might follow in its place is likely to be worse. An ass, belonging to a gardener, worked hard and had little to eat. It prayed to the gods for a change of master. They listened and it was sold to a porter. But the new conditions were even harsher, so it prayed for a further change. The gods now had it sold to a tanner. Too late it realized what was in store for it and it lamented: 'It would have been better to go hungry and carry burdens for my previous owners than to end up here where I shall not even get a burial.' The other fable— already inspected in the chapter on Slaves[3]—takes the opposite line: those at the bottom are unaffected by what goes on at the top, if one ruler replaces the other 'the poor change their master only, not their situation'[4]—hence no loyalty should be expected of them. (Heine's poem König David[5] opens: *Lächelnd scheidet der Despot, denn er weiss, nach seinem Tod wechselt Willkür nur die Hände, und die Knechtschaft hat kein Ende.*) An ass was urged by its owner to run away with him as hostile soldiers were approaching who would otherwise seize it. It asked whether if captured, it would have to carry two packs at a time. To which its master replied: 'Well, no—one pack.' 'Then,' said the beast, 'what difference does it make whom I serve?'

The Hebrews in Egypt would welcome any alternative. They could not be worse off than they are. But there is no need for them to wait for the chance of a war: God has other ways of bringing about their liberation.

Moses's career opens with the killing of an Egyptian overseer for beating up a Hebrew. From the Bible's point of view it is a praiseworthy deed, a sort of anticipation of what is to follow.

---

[1] See below, pp. 129, 130, 133 f., 139, 141, 142 f.
[2] Perry, *Aesopica*, I, 1952, pp. 391 f., summarized by Perry, *Babrius and Phaedrus (Loeb Classical Library)*, 1965, p. 455.
[3] It is by Phaedrus, I.15: Perry, *Babrius and Phaedrus (Loeb Classical Library)*, 1965, p. 210. See above, Children and Slaves, pp. 54 f.
[4] *Nil praeter dominum, non res mutant pauperes*; instead of *dominum, non res* we may have to read *domini mores* or *dominum, cives*—it does not affect my argument.
[5] Elster, *Heinrich Heines sämtliche Werke*, I, p. 356.

Before it comes to the notice of the authorities he escapes into neighbouring Midian. After a while, when there is no longer any danger of discovery, God sends him back from there, to plead with Pharaoh on the people's behalf.

In another lecture,[1] I am adverting to Moses's role as an instance of the fundamental antagonism between prophet and government—foreign or Jewish. At this point, I am concerned with the manner in which the exodus is achieved. At first sight, it could not be more orderly—which is not at all in harmony with the leader's initial proof of his qualifications. Except that to the despotic monarch any suggestion of a lightening of the yoke is offensive, Moses and those in his charge are guilty of no illegality, let alone violence. The worst that happens[2] is that, right at the beginning of his intervention, the Hebrew labourers, in false expectation of an early relenting on the part of the king, slow up on their work or even prepare for a festival. They are soon made to realize their error, their tasks being increased. Actually, they momentarily turn against Moses, accusing him of having made their lot worse instead of better—a typical reaction in this kind of situation and one from which clever rulers know how to profit. For those in power—whether at the helm of a state, guards of a concentration camp, directors of a factory, the Board of the Faculty of Anthropology or the Committee of a country club—it is manifestly of advantage if the bulk of their subjects themselves put down as trouble-makers any from among them who advocate defiance.

No illegality, then, apart from the declared craving for freedom, and no violence. Yet no one ever has looked on the exodus as a model of a sweet and reasonable smoothing away of differences. The explanation is obvious: there is every wildness imaginable, only it emanates from no human source. It is God who causes an invasion of locusts, destructive hailstorms, three days of darkness and, in the end, the death of all the firstborn among the Egyptians—upon which Pharaoh allows, indeed urges, the Hebrews to leave. It should be remembered[3] that, as the Biblical narrator sees it, God comes to the people's

---

[1] On Prophets and Philosophers, p. 64.

[2] Exodus 5.4ff. It is an interesting coincidence that the earliest evidence of strikes in the ancient world comes from Egypt—though about a thousand years after the exodus; see Ziebarth, art.Streik, in Pauly-Wissowa's *Realencyclopädie*, Suppl. 7, 1940, pp. 1250f.

[3] See Daube, *The Exodus Pattern in the Bible*, 1963.

rescue much as, according to a widespread usage of the time, a strong and loyal man would come to the rescue of a relation in distress. If the latter is enslaved, it is the former's right and duty to redeem him—by force if need be; and if the latter is ill-treated, it is the former's right and duty to exact retribution. The Bible represents God as acting in the spirit of those social laws and customs, of immense importance in the ancient world. 'Israel is my son, let my son go,'[1] Pharaoh is told; and as he does not listen, blow follows blow till his will is broken. The victims of oppression may be passive, but their patron is 'a man of war.'[2] As Pharaoh changes his mind and pursues the un-fortunates he has released in order to re-subjugate them, they are assured by Moses: 'The Lord will fight for you.'[3]

We may go further. It is not quite correct to say that the victims are passive. For one thing, most of the disasters which God inflicts on Egypt he has unleashed by a signal from Moses: 'Stretch out thine hand toward heaven that there may be hail.'[4] To be sure, they unmistakably remain expressions of God's power. But when we consider in addition that several of them are terminated by him in response to Moses's entreaty,[5] the latter does appear to exercise some control. The final and most fearful calamity, the slaying of the firstborn, is not initiated by Moses.[6] It is, however, distinguished by another feature here relevant. Before God acts, he bids the Hebrews mark their habitations in order that his wrath should pass them by. For a modern analogy, we might think of an expedition against a state that metes out inhuman treatment to a section of the population: this group is given advance information of a planned air raid and indicates its whereabouts to the bombers with a view to being spared.

One might raise the question how far the very fact that Moses and his flock know of and look forward to the approach of each plague brands them as guilty towards their masters. No doubt in general what goes on inside the mind or soul does not count as a crime. It is well, however, to recognize that, as far as hopes

---

[1] Exodus 4.22f.   [2] Exodus 15.3.   [3] Exodus 14.14.
[4] Exodus 9.22. Sometimes Aaron shares in the procedure, *e.g.*, 7.19.
[5] Exodus 8.8, 26, 9.33, 10.18.
[6] Neither are the fourth and fifth plagues, flies and murrain, Exodus 8.16ff. and 9.1ff. It is, I believe, only in the case of the tenth plague that the omission of the usual gesture by Moses is significant, intended to set this event apart. But I cannot prove it.

and desires are concerned, civil disobedience—and even un-willing compliance—can be highly aggressive, indeed mur-derous. The saint who has the certainty that heaven will fell his adversary looks more irenic than he is. No wonder the other side is apt to get exasperated.

2

The establishment of the Northern Kingdom[1] also is not easy to classify: I incline to assign it to violence. On Solomon's death, the Northern tribes met his son Rehoboam at their centre Shechem and informed him that their allegiance was condi-tional on his undertaking to relax his father's rule; in particular, it seems, they wanted a mitigation of the corvée, the statute labour due to the sovereign. Rehoboam first consulted with the old ministers, who advised accommodation—whether of a genuine kind or meant to deceive the petitioners it is difficult to gather from the text. ('If thou wilt be a servant unto this people this day and wilt serve them and answer them and speak good words to them then they will be thy servants for ever.'[2] While this may be a recommendation of honest concessions, it could mean that the king should show himself conciliatory only in order to get over the present crisis but revert to Solomon's methods later on.) However, he then asked his younger associ-ates. They urged him to give an uncompromising reply, and this is what he did. The Northern tribes thereupon refused to install him, declared their independence of the Davidic house and left Shechem.

So far at least the incident, one might feel, was civil. Yet already it was full of menace. It is enough to observe that it was Jeroboam under whose leadership the Northerners confronted Solomon's son. Jeroboam had attempted, or been thought to attempt, a rebellion against Solomon and had escaped with his life only by taking refuge in Egypt.[3] The Northern tribes, about to assemble at Shechem, summoned him back and he followed their call. That cannot have been interpreted by Re-hoboam as a gesture of moderation.[4]

---

[1] I Kings 12, II Chronicles 10f., 12.6f.
[2] I Kings 12.7. The formulation in II Chronicles 10.7 differs some-what. It does not contain the phrase 'this day' which could (though it need not) imply a yielding for the moment only.
[3] I Kings 11.26ff.
[4] Maybe in an earlier stratum of the tradition Jeroboam was not present

Anyhow, the latter decided to assert his authority and sent his minister managing the corvée to draft the recalcitrants. But the minister was stoned to death. Nor was this an ill-considered deed in hot blood and without further significance. The situation was such that Rehoboam himself had to flee to Jerusalem. When the Northern tribes proclaimed Jeroboam their king, Rehoboam gathered an army but, warned by a prophet that the events had been willed by God, disbanded it again. This, too, reflects no truly peaceful arrangement. Very likely it turned out that Jeroboam could reckon with help from Egypt—if only because a falling apart of the Davidic-Solomonic empire was greatly in that country's interest; so Rehoboam's prospect of success became negligible.[1] We saw above,[2] in discussing the position of the Hebrews under Pharaoh, that the victims of an oppressive regime may find in an external enemy of the latter the martial strength they lack. A few years later, Shishak, the Egyptian ruler who had granted Jeroboam asylum, did invade both Judah and the Northern Kingdom.[3]

There are two more notices in the Bible which must be taken into account if we are to form a realistic picture. First, we are told that though Rehoboam gave up his plan of winning back the North, fighting between him and Jeroboam went on throughout their reigns[4]—presumably border skirmishes, raids and counter-raids. Secondly, Rehoboam's son and successor Abijah (or Abijam) seems to have made a major effort to wrest the North from Jeroboam.[5] In sum, the disruption was rather a high-handed, warlike affair.

---

at the meeting and was put in charge only when this ended in disagreement; see MacLean, art. Jeroboam, in *The Interpreter's Dictionary of The Bible*, 1962, 2, p. 840.

[1] See MacLean, art. Rehoboam, in *The Interpreter's Dictionary*, 4, pp. 29f.

[2] Pp. 124f.

[3] I Kings 14.25 f., II Chronicles 12.2 ff. The Bible mentions the invasion of Judah only, but an Egyptian inscription proves that this is only part of the story; see MacLean, p. 30.

[4] I Kings 14.30, 15.6, II Chronicles 12.15.

[5] I Kings 15.7, II Chronicles 13.3 ff.

3

In the early fifth century BC, the struggle between the orders at Rome reached a climax. At least that is how the sources present it. They may be wildly inaccurate. But I had better announce right away that the problem of historicity will rank very low in this survey, primarily designed to find out, in a general way, how the ancients reacted to certain critical phases of an independence movement. One day it will be possible to be far more exact and discriminating. I shall tackle historicity only where absolutely necessary.

According to Livy then[1]—who wrote under Augustus— in 494 BC the plebeians, the inferior though larger section of the community, decided that, unless there was a drastic change, they would not stay on in the city; and the soldiers among them did leave and encamped on the Sacred Mount near by. No aggression, simply withdrawal. The patricians, the ruling, aristocratic minority, were greatly upset: Rome was engaged in warfare at that moment. They sent a delegation to the separatists to persuade them to return. A fable told by one of the emissaries, Menenius Agrippa, did the trick.[2]

Once upon a time, when man's members were able each to think and speak for itself, the belly seemed to the others to enjoy an outrageous advantage: all the rest worked hard while it sat passively in the middle, just letting itself be fed. They resolved to go on strike. But soon, they found themselves grow weaker and weaker, and it became clear to them that the stomach performed a great task: the food it received, it distributed as rich blood fairly throughout the body. Menenius's hearers acknowledged the analogy to the relationship between plebeians and patricians and agreed to negotiate a reconciliation.

We may leave it open whether the fable really dates from that first plebeian secession or is a subsequent invention. In either case, it is a masterpiece from the point of view of the haves, threatened by an opting out on the part of the have-nots. It deserves careful study.

Before probing it, we should be aware of the significance of the very fact that the plebeians were won over by a fable. At least the circles shaping the tradition behind Livy looked down on this genre. I have already pointed out that it was popular

---

[1] 2.21 ff.   [2] 2.32.8 ff.

among the slaves.[1] The plebeians of that period, we are given to understand, were uncouth enough to respond to this kind of thing; and Menenius who, though on the senatorial side, was of plebeian descent, knew their primitive level of culture. One is left with the feeling that it would not have worked the other way round.[2]

(In 117 AD a popular uprising was prevented by the telling of an Aesopic fable.[3] Hadrian had recently come to the throne and had got Jewish rebels to lay down their arms in return for a promise that the Temple would be restored. Once his object was reached, however, he went back on his word, whereupon a fresh revolt threatened to break out.[4] Rabbi Joshua ben Hananiah, then an octogenarian, pacified the belligerent spirits by relating an encounter between a lion and an Egyptian partridge, a bird with a particularly long beak. The lion had eaten up an animal, and a bone stuck in his throat. He promised a huge reward to whoever would rid him of that terrible thing. The partridge did so, but when he asked for the reward, the lion retorted that he should be well satisfied having escaped from his jaws unharmed. It was enough, Rabbi Joshua concluded, to get off in peace from any dealing with the Romans; and the people listened to him. It is interesting that the rabbi, like Menenius Agrippa, acted as an emissary—the Sages who were averse to a renewal of warfare sent him to the populace[5]—and, like Agrippa, was of a lowly background, a charcoal-burner or a smith.[6]

The Midrash attaches the anecdote to a statement which, according to Genesis,[7] a Philistine king made to Abraham: 'We

---

[1] Above, Children and Slaves, pp. 53 ff.

[2] Livy 2.32.8 remarks that Menenius was dear to the plebs *quod inde oriundus erat*; and that *prisco illo dicendi et horrido modo nihil aliud quam hoc narasse fertur*.

[3] Genesis Rabba 64 on Genesis 26.29. Greek versions of the fable are found in Halm, *Fabulae Aesopicae Collectae*, 1911, pp. 135f., Perry, *Aesopica*, 1, 1952, p. 382, and Perry, *Babrius and Phaedrus* (*Loeb Classical Library*), 1965, p. 115 (Babrius no. 94); a Latin one in the last-mentioned work, p. 201 (Phaedrus 1.8).

[4] See Graetz, *Geschichte des Jüdischen Volkes*, 4, 4th ed., pp. 125, 129, 408, 414.

[5] Because, we are told, he was a *scholastikos*, an expert, an advocate, of the Torah; the Midrash uses the Greek term (see Krauss, *Griechische und Lateinische Lehnwörter in Talmud, Midrasch und Targum*, 2, 1899, p. 87).

[6] Babylonian Berakoth 28 a.   [7] 26.29.

have not touched thee, and have done unto thee only good and have sent thee away in peace.' This heathen ruler was here admitting—that is how the Midrash interprets him—that, for the likes of him, to refrain from hurt was the height of benevolence: the non-touching and the dismissing-in-peace constitute the good done. It is quite possible that whoever connected the episode of Rabbi Joshua with this verse knew the fable also from another source, i.e. from that Greek one which expressly supplies the moral that the best treatment to be expected from the wicked is not to be injured by them.[1])

Unlike the two fables I quoted earlier on,[2] one about an ass achieving a change of master and finding itself worse off than before, one about an ass indifferent for whom it labours, this one purposes to refute subjects fed up with being subjects. Those two asses know that they are and will always be asses: the only problem is whether to stick to the present master. Menenius's addressees are no longer willing to remain subservient.

That his fable is directed against non-violent conduct is evident: the complaining members inflict no hurt on the belly, which would make a quick, satisfactory resumption of co-operation difficult. They simply abstain from their business. Their main charge as such is not denied: the belly does swallow the delectable things their labour provides. What they are said to have overlooked is that though that organ depends on them—this is admitted—they in turn depend on it: in a superior, refined, inconspicuous fashion it, too, is active for the common good, actually more universally needed than any of the malcontents. The upshot is that no fundamental change will ever be possible: the respective functions of the various parts of the body are interlocking and fixed, and that of the stomach is the most indispensable of all. In one form or another, this argumentation recurs throughout the ages, wherever the hungry many are to be discouraged from encroaching on the exclusive rights of the few.

---

[1] See Halm, p. 136, Perry, *Aesopica*, I, p. 382: 'with evil-doers the greatest requital of a kindness is not to be further wronged by them'. The Greek and Latin texts, incidentally, speak of a wolf, not a lion. I suppose Hadrian was more appropriately compared to the latter. The Egyptian partridge—as distinct from heron or crane—is no doubt introduced in order to make matters familiar and lively.

[2] Above, p. 125.

It is, of course, disingenuous. To reflect on the similarity between a social structure and an anatomical one can be quite
stimulating; to treat them as the same is a different matter. I
shall be content with pointing out two tricks involved in this
fable. First, the human body does perish without a stomach: an
organization may or may not perish without its elite. Menenius's audience might have replied that one could think of
other methods of direction. Secondly, even granted that an
elite of the present type is essential, the anatomical comparison
is misleading. The function of my stomach can be performed
only by my stomach, not by my feet, that of my feet only by my
feet, not by my stomach; whereas in a social system, even if the
various functions as such are indispensable, they can often be
performed by one person or group as efficiently as by another.
My feet cannot digest, my stomach cannot walk; whereas a
judicious change of places between inferiors and superiors in a
polity need not be ruinous. Menenius's audience could have retorted: 'Right, there must be a belly as well as other parts, only
let us be the belly for a spell and undertake the refined tasks,
while the senators labour as eyes, hands and feet.'

(There is another perennial line to maintain the status quo—
the contention that the have-nots would not appreciate or even
tolerate the luxuries of the haves. This, too, is set forth in a
fable about the body: the eyes envied the mouth the honey it
was fed, but when they were given some, they smarted and
found it repellent. Dio Chrysostom, from whom we know this
fancy—which he ascribes to Aesop[1]—likens his philosophy to
honey and his audience to eyes: they may not like what he has
to say to them. 'They put coal into the bathtub,' used to be
said about poor immigrants to England not so long ago.)[2]

As one might guess, it is especially at moments when the
goodwill of the masses is badly wanted that they are reminded
of the concerns common to all and the pettiness of group interests, *Sonderinteressen*. Rome was at war when Menenius gave
his address. In August 1914, the Emperor William II proclaimed: 'I no longer know any parties, I know Germans only,'
and again, 'Never yet was Germany defeated when she was

---

[1] 33.16. Perry (*Transactions of the American Philological Association*, 93,
1962, pp. 314f.) suggests that Dio Chrysostom found it in the collection
of Demetrius of Phalerum—a highly elitist mind around 300 BC.
[2] It would lead too far afield here to connect the two fables with major
doctrines concerning the nature of man or natures of men.

united.'[1] The phrases 'we are all in the same boat' and 'do not rock the boat' are pleas preferred during a dangerous voyage by those who have most to gain from safe arrival in port.[2] They are not readily translatable into other languages—even if we are prepared to give up the connection with the sea. The nearest German I can think of would be far more abstract: *wir sind auf Gedeih und Verderb verbunden*, 'we are bound together for salvation or perdition'—though this, too, will normally be an appeal of the few to the many.[3] Maybe the existence of the English idiom betokens a closeness of the British political genius to the Roman.

Scholars are strangely oblivious of the particular point of the fable. As a result, they list ever so many sources, Oriental, Greek, Roman and Christian, which, they believe, contain the same story or vestiges of it—often wrongly, it turns out on inspection. A footnote by the translator of Livy in the Loeb edition is typical: 'The same apologue is found in Xenophon, *Memorabilia*, Cicero, *de Officiis*, and St Paul, I Corinthians.'[4] In reality, of the three, only Paul is likely to have it in mind; even here some doubt remains.

Let us look at them. Xenophon depicts Socrates as advocating friendship between two quarrelling brothers. What if a pair of hands or feet, made for mutual help, took to thwarting one another? That is how at present they behave. No doubt in this simile, as in that of Menenius, the members of the body are

---

[1] *Ich kenne keine Parteien mehr, ich kenne nur noch Deutsche. Noch nie ward Deutschland überwunden, wenn es einig war.* See Büchmann, *Geflügelte Worte*, 26th ed. by Krieger, 1920, pp. 584f.

[2] The latest instance that has come to my notice is found in the *San Francisco Chronicle* on May 2, 1971, p. 28. Mayor Alioto said: 'The basic acceptance of Teilhard by atheists, agnostics, Marxists and eminent churchmen . . . may well be the instrument for unifying many in the world who have lived in antagonism to each other and suddenly discovered they are in the same boat.'

[3] Langenscheidt's *New Muret-Sanders*, Pt. 1, English-German, ed. Springer, 1963, p. 1199, renders 'to rock the boat' by *die Sache ins Wanken bringen*, 'to make the matter shake.' This does not do the English justice.

[4] Foster, *Livy*, I, 1919, p. 324. The full references are *Memorabilia* 2.3.4, *de Officiis* 3.5.22, I Corinthians 12.12. Of course, no commentator would rule out differences in detail between Livy and versions of the fable drawn on by others. Xenophon, for example, centuries before Livy, would not be expected by anyone to know the fable in precisely the form it has in *Ab Urbe Condita*.

personified and used to illustrate the wisdom of nature-designed concord and the absurdity of discord. But the problem of privilege is not considered at all, nor is the interest confined to civil resistance—Socrates' conclusion would follow even more obviously if one hand or foot did serious harm to the other. The situation he is envisaging and the ends he is pursuing are quite different from those in the fable; the latter plays no part whatever. In both the fable of the ant and the cicada and that of the fox and the crow we find animals talking to one another and useful qualities praised: yet no one would maintain these two fables are one. To identify Menenius' fable with Xenophon's is no better.

Cicero, it is safe to assume, was acquainted with the former. Nevertheless, the passage alleged to be based on it could be written if he had never heard of it. One reason, he declares, it is wrong to gain by despoiling a fellow-man is that society as a whole is thereby broken up. It is as if each of our members were to try to get stronger by drawing off the strength of its neighbour—the result would be ruin to the entire body. Again, personification of the members; beyond that, not (as in Xenophon) praise of concord and condemnation of discord, but praise of moral self-restraint and condemnation of egotistic disregard of justice. Of the distinctive features of Menenius' fable, not a trace.

When we come to I Corinthians a verdict is less easily reached. Paul exhorts those with special gifts—prophecy, healing, etc.—each to cultivate his variety, at the same time respecting the others.[1] There is value in the contributors of lower services as well as in those of higher ones; together they form the Church, the body of Christ. If the foot or ear were to think that, because it was not a hand or eye, it did not belong to the body, it would nonetheless belong to it. If the whole body were eye, there would be no hearing, if hearing, there would be no smelling. The members are each in the place assigned by God. In fact, the apparently weaker members are indispensable, and the less honourable ones are paid particular honour in that they receive clothing—not required by the seemly ones. God has put the body together and accorded more honour to what is less honourable, in order that there should be no division and that

---

[1] Cp. Daube, in *Jesus and Man's Hope*, ed. Miller and Hadidian, 2, 1971, p. 230.

all members should have the same care for one another. If one of them suffers, all others suffer with it, if one is glorified, all others rejoice with it. Just so, Paul's addressees are the body of Christ, every one of them a member. Some are apostles, some prophets, some teachers, some ecstatic speakers and so on, all of them wanted though those with a humbler gift (like ecstatic speech) should certainly strive to attain a more precious one (like prophecy).

Here indeed, besides personification of the members and insistence on harmony, two of the more peculiar elements of the fable are present. Attention focuses on trouble created by diversity in function, and the complications are non-violent: disappointment on the part of the lowly, pride on the part of the high-ups. Moreover, basically, the solution propounded is not too dissimilar to that of the fable. Some gifts excel others. Yet, they are all essential to one another and to the fabric of the Church as a whole. Hence, you must do your best with whichever you possess.

On the other hand, the Epistle includes important teachings with no parallel, such as the compensatory deference payable to the less seemly members. God himself, Paul suggests, set the example for this when he clothed the first couple,[1] and our covering of the shameful parts is a constant reminder of our duty to the underdog. A weighty deviation from the fable is the demand that the possessors of less valuable gifts should struggle towards more valuable ones: you are not—in the religious sphere at least—rigidly tied to your status, you may, indeed ought to, advance.[2]

---

[1] Genesis 3.21. On the normative force of example, and in particular God's, see Daube, *The New Testament and Rabbinic Judaism*, 1956, pp. 67 ff. Significantly, the rabbis, no less than Paul, treat the action recorded in Genesis 3.21 as directive. The Pentateuch, they observe, begins and ends with a deed of loving-kindness by God: it begins with his clothing the naked and it ends—Deuteronomy 34.6—with his burying the dead, namely Moses. It is up to man to imitate this pattern: Babylonian Sota 14a.

[2] The following chapter 13 goes beyond the traditional, rational ordering of a composite society and proclaims 'a more excellent way' (12.31) unmistakably Pauline: *agape*, love, charity, consideration for one's fellow, caring for him. It is after inculcating this supreme organizing principle that Paul, in chapter 14, feels able to aver in forthright terms, yet without wounding anyone, the inferiority of ecstatic speech as compared with prophecy.

What is intriguing is certain affinities, not directly with the fable, but with ideas which Roman historical tradition—in Livy or Dionysius of Halicarnassus—describes as prominent in the struggle between the orders. In Paul's exposition, the lowly members, feet and ear, feel left out, take the view that, unlike their superiors, hand and eye, they are not integrated in the body. The Roman historians represent the plebeians as claiming that they are cut off,[1] forced out into a separate state,[2] while longing to be united with the patricians,[3] to be of the citizens at large.[4] Conversely, in Paul's exposition, the high-ups, eye and head, look down on their inferiors, hand and feet, as expendable. Appius Claudius, the diehard opposed to any concession to the plebeians, asserts that the patricians can do without them.[5]

On balance, it does look as if Paul in this Epistle were in touch with Menenius' fable and its Roman setting. Surprisingly, his Epistle to the Romans,[6] composed several years later, though resuming the comparison of the Church to body and members, shows none of that influence. There is no explicit reference here to high and low; Paul simply urges that, like the members of the body, the Christians—forming one body in Christ and being members of one another—have different gifts and are each to live up to his. Two factors account for the dropping out of the specific thrust of the fable. For one thing, the discussion in Romans is very much shorter.[7] For another, in Romans the apostle is far less exercised by the danger of splits, schisms, in the community. Preoccupation with this evil in I Corinthians[8] would naturally bring the fable and its circumstances into prominence.

Evidently, awareness of the fable's character is a necessary safeguard against overrating its impact. It also helps us to

---

[1] Dionysius 6.79.1 *diereken hemas*.
[2] Dionysius 6.79.1 *tous demotas ekbalontes*, 6.36.1 *diokismetha kai dys poleis echomen*, Livy 4.4.6 (on a later, similar occasion) *exsilium intra moenia*, 4.4.10 *dirimatis societatem civilem duasque ex una civitate faciatis*, Plutarch, Coriolanus 6.1 *ekpeptokenai tes poleos*.
[3] Livy 4.3.3 *eorum esse*, 4.5.5 *coalescere*.
[4] Livy 4.3.2 *admonemus cives nos eorum esse*.
[5] Dionysius 6.64.2. On another detail of his speech, see below, p. 139.
[6] 12.3 ff.
[7] This comes out also in the rather abrupt introduction of *agape* in 12.9—contrasting with its well-prepared one in I Corinthians 13.
[8] The term *schisma* occurs in 1.10, 11.18 and 12.24.

appreciate the purposeful twist given to a predecessor, an earlier, simpler fable by Aesop.[1] Here the legs boast to the stomach that they are stronger since they carry it, but the stomach replies that, unless it nourished them, they could not do so.

This is a *Rangstreitfabel*, a dispute about rank,[2] and the stomach has the last word—though it is a narrow win. The prowess of the legs is conceded. The main lesson is mutual dependence, with the stomach, however, doing the primary, basic job. The most notable innovation in Menenius' fable is that abstract debate is turned into confrontation and action. The other members do not just remark that they are more useful than the belly. They charge exploitation and attempt to effect a reversal. In turn, the belly does not just deliver a repartee. Its enforced passivity soon compels its detractors to give in and acknowledge the inevitability of the discriminatory set-up. Aesop has neither civil disobedience nor penitent return, both of the utmost importance to Menenius.

That the latter's version is a development from the former's, one would consider probable on general grounds. The matter is certain because a fable close to Aesop's is met in Egypt around 1,000 BC. The stomach goes to law against the head in order to have it pronounced inferior—feeble and weepy. By way of counter-charge, the head claims to be the chief support and life-source of the body.[3] However early a date we put on Menenius' version, that of Aesop, derived from Egypt, must have been current by then throughout the Mediterranean world. Dionysius of Halicarnassus, incidentally, speaks of Menenius' fable as composed in the manner of Aesop.[4]

Aesop's fable is provided with a moral: in the case of armies, numbers are of no avail if the generals do not excel. Whether this military interpretation goes back to the Egyptian stage, it is difficult to say; no explicit moral has come down to us from there. It is not even beyond doubt that Aesop's fable was from

---

[1] Perry, *Aesopica*, I, 1952, pp. 371f. On Aesop's fable of eyes and mouth, see above, p. 133.

[2] See Perry, *Babrius and Phaedrus* (*Loeb Classical Library*), 1965, pp. XXVIf.

[3] It seems (see Brunner-Traut, *Altägyptische Märchen*, 1963, p. 279) that, originally at least, no social application was intended: the tale was concerned solely with the relation between the different parts of the human anatomy.

[4] 6.83.2.

the outset so understood. However, quite likely it was; and if not, it must have been before long. The army is the most glaring instance of the rule of a few over many; sociologists commonly refer to it as exemplifying the master-subject or domination-submission type of order.[1]

Menenius at any rate recounts the story in a definitely military context. Rome is at this moment at war with dangerous neighbours, and it is the plebeian soldiers—constituting the bulk of the forces—who turn their backs on their patrician leaders and pitch their tents on the Sacred Mount. Clearly, though he means to illumine the entire relationship between the orders, the immediate question before him is the respective positions of troops and generals: the former, however indignant with the latter, ought to return to their posts. Again, in the declamation put into the mouth of Appius Claudius by Dionysius, while the fable is not mentioned, its military moral may well be behind the final argument against yielding to the secessionists: though Rome is at war, the old reactionary maintains, she has no need of numbers, being blessed with outstanding generals.[2] We must bear in mind that, over the years, Roman thinkers would tend to transfer the fable's message from the military field to the commonwealth in general: the narrower scope is thereby obscured, but it is the original one.

Paul in I Corinthians makes no allusion to a military association of the simile of body and members. Some forty years later, however, the author of I Clement,[3] like Paul dealing with factions in the Corinthian Church and drawing on Paul's I Corinthians,[4] does prefix to the simile a reference to military discipline. He opens this section by calling attention to the ready execution in an army of the commands of the generals and to the hierarchy of officers, from brigadier down to lieutenant, each in his station carrying out the orders of the Emperor and generals. Then he goes on to what is enunciated in Paul: the interdependence of head and feet, the value of any member, however minor, to the body in its totality, and the analogous

---

[1] The typology in question is put to use in the field of legal philosophy by Coing, *Grundzüge der Rechtsphilosophie*, 1950, pp. 69 ff.
[2] 6.64.1 f. The logic is less than perfect. After explaining that numbers do not matter, Appius goes on to point out that good generals attract recruits, so the deserters will quickly be replaced by men returning from the colonies, loyal Latins volunteering and so on.
[3] In 37 f.   [4] I Corinthians is expressly cited in I Clement 47.1.

situation of a Christian community. This introduction, or re-introduction, of the military application of the fable is one of the numerous displays by I Clement of wider, Hellenistic culture on top of specific Christian (here: Pauline) tradition.[1]

I shall not dwell on the selection of bodily parts in the successive presentations of a conflict between them; to do so profitably would necessitate an excursus into archaic medicine. One aspect only I would single out. The equation of the greedy belly with the generals has a very concrete basis: in most ancient systems it is they to whom belonged all major war booty, *Grossbeute*, even though, at Rome at least, they were expected to hand over part of it to the treasury. It is worth noting that, immediately before the first secession, a pro-plebeian general named Servilius had permitted his soldiers to appropriate the entire booty of a campaign, for which subversive measure the senate, at the instance of Appius Claudius, refused him the customary victor's triumph. He celebrated it regardless—an enormous act of civil disobedience by a patrician, preceding the plebeian exodus.[2]

As the moral of the fable is being extended beyond the military area, one can notice a gradual replacement of the stomach by the head; it is the latter that lords it over the rest.[3] The shift is detectable in Dionysius.[4] Valerius Maximus, without express reference to the fable but surely aware of it, deplores the secession as cutting off part of the body of the state (the plebeians) from its head (the patricians).[5] There is no mention of the stomach either in I Corinthians or in I Clement; both mention the head and in I Corinthians it and the eye are warned not to despise hands and feet.[6] To attack the rulers as the belly is

---

[1] For a characterisation of the Epistle, see Harnack, *Einführung in die Alte Kirchengeschichte, Das Schreiben der Römischen Kirche an die Korinthische aus der Zeit Domitians*, 1929, pp. 58, 76, 83.

[2] Dionysius 6.29.4f., 30.2, 44.1. On the Roman law concerning booty, see Vogel, *Zeitschrift der Savigny-Stiftung*, **66**, 1948, Rom. Abt., pp. 394ff. The case of Servilius is noted on pp. 415f.

[3] It may be recalled that, in an Egyptian text of 1,000 B C (above, p. 138), it is stomach and head that are rivals. The head, however, does not here stand for sovereignty and direction. Its chief pride is the life-mediating nose, while the stomach boasts of receiving and distributing food.

[4] In his version of the fable, the head no less than the stomach 'preserves', *sozo*, the whole body: 6.86.2, 5. 'Preservation' is, of course, the job of the patrician senate: 6.86.5.

[5] 8.9.1; more on this writer below, pp. 148ff.

[6] I Corinthians 12.21, I Clement 37.5.

directly to object to the unfair gains they make by their position. To attack them as the head is more abstract, it is to object
to their position—though, of course, in view of the gains they
derive from it. The transition implies an advance in theory, also
in gentility, and a corresponding loss in honesty. The rulers
certainly prefer to debate on the more intellectual plane—*i.e.*,
to justify their headship—to debating on the cruder one—*i.e.*,
to justifying their bellyship; and an opponent who harps on the
latter is regarded as particularly offensive, vulgar. Goethe's
line *Die Kirche hat einen guten Magen*, 'The Church has a good
digestion' (literally, 'a good stomach'), is very hard-hitting.[1]

Paradoxically, in a way, the renunciation of violence by the
dissident plebeians chimes with the military background. In
war, you may destroy those who rely on you by standing aside
no less rapidly and thoroughly than by going for them. There is
not much that military authority fears more than refusal of
subordinates to obey—mere refusal. The Swiss code of military law allows the death penalty if this offence takes place at the
front.[2] Actually, what is true of war is true of any life-and-death
struggle. When, at the approach of the insurrectional legions
under Galba, the Emperor Nero's retainers and guards deserted him, his doom was sealed.[3] One of the grandest scenes
in the Icelandic saga of Burnt Njal occurs as the peerless
Gunnar defends his homestead single-handedly against a horde
of enemies. The string of his bow is cut by one of them, and he
asks his wife—famous for her hair—for two of her locks which
could be twisted so as to replace it. But she, ever remembering a
deep slight he inflicted on her long before, declines the request
and he is overwhelmed and killed.[4]

This is not to minimize the difference, even in such circumstances, between forsaking and active hostilities. I cannot here

---

[1] *Faust*, Erster Teil, Spaziergang. It is wrapped up most carefully:
put into the mouth of Mephistopheles, who reports it as coming from a
pious cleric explaining to Gretchen and her mother that the jewelry
which has turned up in the former's room should be dedicated to the
Virgin Mary. Almost as many layers as in the Lorelei, where the poet is
sad because he remembers a tale where a maiden sings a strange song
which makes a man in a boat sad. Goethe would not be caught out by
the establishment. Heine would not be caught out by himself.
[2] *Schweizerisches Militärstrafgesetzbuch* of 1927, art. 61.
[3] Suetonius, Nero 47.2f.
[4] Dasent, *The Story of Burnt Njal*, 1861, i, pp. 245f. The slapping
of her face is on p. 153.

go into the vast subject of direct and indirect causation or the related one of commission and omission. To see the point, we need only imagine one of Nero's courtiers stabbing him to death or the Icelandic lady Hallgerda giving her husband poison. In the Second Book of Samuel, a rebel against King David makes his last stand in a city, surrounded by an over-whelming force. The inhabitants, in order to avoid disaster, throw his head over the wall to the besiegers. That is not the same as if they had simply ceased aiding him and left him to his fate.[1] In the case of the first plebeian secession, the disaffected troops actually reunited with the rest before the enemies of Rome could bring off a major blow. Still, it is always good to bear in mind that civil disobedience may be exercised in a fashion bringing it very close to violence.

As remarked above,[2] war can be a unifier, namely, if the dis-satisfied group hates the foreign adversary more than the native one. In fact, the latter may engineer a war on purpose to avoid being overthrown. According to Dionysius,[3] that is what the consuls did in the year before this secession: they attacked the Volscians, since 'it would be of the greatest benefit to divert the intramural uproar to external wars.' (Livy, too, knows of this sort of thing.[4]) The scheme, however, was only partially successful, the bulk of the populace flouting the summons to enlist. Where the native oppressor is insufferable, a war, far from silencing the down-trodden, will encourage them to assert themselves. During several decades, we find the plebeians evading the levy[5] or, in the field, refusing to fight[6] or fighting only in defence of the stockade:[7] an amazing range of pressure. They did draw the line at making common cause with the enemy—though the patricians feared[8] and the enemy hoped[9]

---

[1] II Samuel 20.14ff. See Daube, *Collaboration with Tyranny in Rabbinic Law*, 1965, pp. 20ff.

[2] P. 124.

[3] 6.23.1; cp. Livy 2.23.1. From Greek history, cp. *e.g.* Plutarch, *Pericles* 32.3.

[4] E.g.,4.1.4f.,about the events of 445 BC, when the plebeians demanded access to the office of consul.

[5] Livy 2.24.2, 27.10, 28.5f., 43.3—by this time one can speak of 'the custom of refusing the call to arms,' *mos detractandi militiam*—4.5.6,6.5.

[6] 2.45.7ff.   [7] 2.59.3.

[8] Dionysius 6.47.1f. The fear may be implied by Livy 2.32.6: 'What might happen if some foreign war should break out in the meantime?'

[9] Livy 2.58.3.

they might, so that extreme course was not out of the question.

They did not resort to it. The choice by the Roman chroniclers of the verb *secedere*[1] and the noun *secessio*[2] to denote the plebeian withdrawals emphasizes this aspect. These words, in contradistinction to others like *deficere*, *defectio*, exclude the ultimate betrayal. One can *deficere ad hostem*, 'defect to the enemy'; one cannot, in Latin, *secedere ad hostem*, 'secede to the enemy', just as in English one would not 'break away to somebody' or 'drop out to somebody'. A secession, to be sure, may be a greater threat to the commonwealth than many a defection. But, morally, it is on a higher level, not utterly ignoble. *Deficere* and *defectio* do occur in connection with one secession, undertaken in 342 BC by the troops at Capua; I shall point out the implications of this below.[3]

The striving for terminology upholding the plebeians' fundamental patriotism is intense. Florus—writing in the reign of Hadrian—in his summary of Menenius' fable refers to a *seiunctio*, 'disjointedness,' of the rebellious members from the stomach.[4] *Seiunctio* is exceedingly rare; it may well figure here because, like *secessio*, it means separation as such; it is never 'to the enemy'. Of particular significance is the lack of Greek equivalents of *secedere* and *secessio* in the political sense. Forcellini's lexicon offers *apochoreo* and *apochoresis*. This pair would indeed have a similar flavour; but I cannot find it in any ancient account of the Roman troubles. Dionysius consistently employs *aphistanai*[5] and *apostasis*,[6] the usual terms for 'to revolt, defect' and 'a revolt, defection',[7] and let us note that one can *aphistanai pros polemion*, 'defect to the enemy'. Twentieth-century German scholars, incidentally, now and then translate *secessio* by *Wehrstreik*, 'draftees' strike'—sometimes in inverted commas.[8] (Over a glass of wine, Lysistrata and her sisters may be said to have gone on *Wehrstreik*.) This rendering falls in with the Roman assessment: it contains no hint at *Landesverrat*, joining up with a foreign power.

It was the first secession which set a precedent in the scorning

---

[1] *E.g.*, Livy 2.32.2, 6.
[2] *E.g.*,2.58.3. In this very passage Livy, however, mentions the expectation of the Volscians that the seceding troops might come over to them.
[3] P. 147.   [4] 1.17.23.2.   [5] 6.45.2.   [6] 6.45.1.
[7] They occur, for instance, in connection with defections from the Delian League in Thucydides 1.98f. (Naxos), 1.115.5 (Samos).
[8] See *e.g.*, Bengtson, *Grundriss der Römischen Geschichte*, 1967, p. 37.

of defection even when taking the unheard of step of moving out. We have already seen[1] that, as depicted in Roman literature, it also provided an example of principled abstention from violence and destruction. The campers on the Sacred Mount had to help themselves to food from the fields near their tents; but they seized a minimum, laid hands on no one and indeed, as Livy puts it, 'would neither take nor give offence':[2] a star case of civil disobedience. Forty-five years later, in the second secession, those marching out, we are told, 'imitated the modesty of their fathers and committed no outrage.'[3] Yet again, when another century had passed, both the secessionist garrison of Capua and the authorities whom they had offended were exhorted by well-wishers to emulate the decency of their respective predecessors.[4]

As often, much depends on the spectacles worn by the observer. Roman tradition could have fastened on different details, could have set up the first secession as the prototype of fierce revolution. After all, ugly scenes occurred not only prior to the soldiers putting up their unauthorized encampment,[5] but also when the patricians closed the city-gates in order to prevent the plebeians inside from reinforcing the mutineers on the Mount.[6] Moreover, all the time the latter made it abundantly clear that they would resist by force of arms any attempt to bring them back under lawful rule against their will.[7] A striking passage occurs in Livy's account of the second secession: as the decemvirs rushed through the army, hoping to restore order, 'to such as remonstrated mildly no answer was given—if any tried to use his authority he was told that those before him were men and armed.'[8] In the course of Roman history, dire punishment was meted out for far less.[9]

To concentrate on the civil features was desirable, first, because there was a happy end, a mending of the estrangement,

---

[1] Above, p. 130.
[2] 2.32.4, *neque lacessiti neque lacessentes.* Cp. Dionysius 6.46.2, Plutarch, *Coriolanus* 6.1.
[3] Livy 3.52.3: *modestiam patrum suorum nihil violando imitati.*
[4] Livy 7.40.11, 41.2.
[5] Creditors were manhandled, Livy 2.27.9, even senators were pushed around (though no weapons were used), 2.29.4.
[6] Dionysius 6.46.1 f.   [7] *E.g.*, Dionysius 6.73.1.
[8] 3.50.12: *leniter agentibus responsum non redditur, imperium si quis inhiberet et viros et armatos se esse respondetur.*
[9] *E.g.* Valerius Maximus 6.3.4; see Mommsen, *Römisches Strafrecht*, 1899, p. 44.

which must not be marred by unpleasant memories; and secondly, because it was hoped the masses would accept the peaceful method as an ideal, a model. (You must have noticed that when your cur threatens to be obstreperous, a fairly reliable way of calming him is to address him: 'good, little doggie'.) It is true that the conservative bias of our principal sources, Livy and Dionysius of Halicarnassus, makes for a one-sided picture. The latter, with an alien's exaggerated reverence, makes a sweeping statement which is contradicted as one probes into his own exposition: such was the spirit of harmony in ancient Rome, he affirms, that in six-hundred-and-thirty years —*i.e.*, till Gaius Gracchus—no bloodshed ever accompanied political controversy.[1] But Livy is not much less eulogistic of the past.[2] Very likely there were circles that did not play down the radical phases of the secessions to the same extent. But their accounts have not survived.

For the followers of the orthodox line, precisely because they believed in the genuine, sacred unity of the nation, the secessions, civil though they were, had the most fearful, unnatural impact. Valerius Maximus says that 'the condition of the state, when the rest of the body was divided from its head by a baleful sedition, was both misshapen and most wretched.'[3] In my second lecture on Women, I mention Cato's denunciation of the ladies fighting the Oppian law which restricted their expense, and his likening of their unruly behaviour to the plebeian secessions.[4] It is a gross exaggeration, yet it reflects this feeling about the secessions that, monstrously, part of your very self, a group you had counted on as inseparably attached, turned against you.

I wonder whether some of the rhetoric of the secessions may not be considerably influenced by that of colonization. The sending out of a number of fellow-citizens to settle elsewhere was a peaceful enterprise, but it often had a tragic quality—as

---

[1] 2.11.2. Cp. my *Roman Law*, 1969, pp. 80, 120f.

[2] See his reflections in the section about the mutiny at Capua, 7.40.2, cp. 7.40.12.

[3] 8.9.1: *eratque non solum deformis sed etiam miserrimus rei publicae status, a capite eius cetera parte corporis pestifera seditione divisa.* He refers to *plebs dissidens*, 'the dissident plebs': no allusion to defection. The ugly appearance of a body from which a portion is lopped off is mentioned also by Dionysius 6.54.2.

[4] See The Women of Rome, pp. 28f.; Livy 34.2.7.

when a primary motive was famine. To go by Roman tradition, in the first quarter of the fourth century BC, had the indigent inhabitants of Rome had their way, a good half of them would have chosen to colonize Veii—an Etruscan place recently conquered.[1]

Another motive occasionally met is here of interest: the wish to get rid of awkward components of the population. It is noteworthy that, immediately before the first secession, the dictator Valerius, having conquered some Volscian territory, had it occupied by poor people, in order to reduce the revolutionary element at home.[2] If a man whose sympathies were with the plebeians could act like this, we can imagaine the policies of the anti-plebeian wing. Actually, one proposal reported to have emanated from that side during the first secession[3] was to consider the plebeians a good riddance and invite labourers and suchlike folk from surrounding tribes to settle at Rome in the place of those who had left.

Hence, when Dionysius represents the secessionists as exclaiming, 'We shall be content with any land, wherever it may be, in which we may have freedom'[4]—and there are many laments of this nature in the course of the several secessions—Roman ears may well have picked up an echo from the partings of emigrants to colonies. In one speech a plebeian leader expressly introduces this situation: 'We, abandoning this life without city and without hearth, go forth as a colony.'[5]

The attribution to a movement of a civil character or a violent one is, I maintain, to a high degree subjective. Let me now add that even its subsumption under or exclusion from the heading secession may be based on the classifier's attitude as much as on objective data. Modern authorities are apt to forget about this. In 343 BC Capua placed itself under Roman protection. A year later,[6] the Roman garrison, contrary to the directions of its commanders, prepared to seize the city and settle there with their families, freed at last from the poverty and disabilities they were suffering at home. An armed clash with the regiment despatched against them from Rome was narrowly avoided; unity was restored.

In modern literature, one comes across such statements as that, no matter what the sources say, the incident was 'merely a

---

[1] Livy 5.24.5ff., 49.8.   [2] Dionysius 6.43.1.   [3] Dionysius 6.52.1f.
[4] 6.45.1.   [5] 6.80.3: *stellomen apoikian*.   [6] Livy 7.38ff.

military rebellion.'[1] But Livy does call it 'a secession', and in this he manifestly represents an official tradition: a law granting the soldiers amnesty contained this term.[2] (That law alone is adequate proof that his use of the word is not metaphorical, as it is in Cato's tirade against female luxuries.[3]) The involvement of a large body of troops with complaints about usury and other oppression at Rome, their intention of seeking their fortunes abroad and the ending of the affair by negotiation led the contemporaries to consider 'secession' the appropriate description. (The affinity of secession and colonization, incidentally, seems well illustrated by this incident, where Capua was the prize coveted.) Any criticism—and why should there be none?— ought to take the form: for them, proceeding from such and such premises, it was secession, for us, with different premises, it was not. Future historians may argue that the Britain of the nineteen-seventies was no longer a monarchy; it is to be hoped that they will still recognize the importance of the label prevalent today.

In one respect already Livy treats the case somewhat differently from the previous ones: he refers to it as 'a defection'.[4] We know that this upheaval did have very adverse effects on the wars and near-wars on which Rome was then engaged: several allies fell away and there were serious incursions into Roman-held regions.[5] Moreover, the rebels of Capua did resort to disorderly pillages.[6] These matters, we must remember, were better documented than the half-mythological secessions of the fifth century BC and, therefore, more difficult to romanticize. I suppose 'secession' reflects the prudently conciliatory language of those who had to deal with the mutineers, 'defection' a less sparing judgement which became increasingly vocal.

That the official moderation was from the first not to everybody's taste is shown by a curious measure taken on top of the amnesty. The dictator formally begged the assembled citizens

---

[1] Treves, art. Secessio, in *Oxford Classical Dictionary*, 2nd ed., 1970, p. 969.
[2] Livy 7.41.3: *ne cui militum fraudi esset secessio*. At the very least, this must have been an early resumé of the law.
[3] Livy 34.2.7. Even Cato's consciously rhetorical application is far from nonsensical. See above, p. 145.
[4] 7.42.2, *defectio*. The verb *deficere* is found in the post-Livian summary of his Book 7, towards the end.
[5] Livy 7.42.8.   [6] Livy 7.39.9.

—thereby making it a point of honour and religion—to reproach no participant in this sedition even in jest.[1] Passions must have been running high indeed. I can recall no comparable public resolution though, presumably, certain restrictions on satire—whether prose, poetry, song or comedy—are founded on a similar rationale. Another development is suggestive: it looks as if some major concessions made to the mutineers at the time[2] were gradually pushed into the background by the annalists, given less and less mention—surely *pour décourager les autres*. No good could come of revealing to the ignorant that disloyalty might, with luck, pay off.

The sources refer to five secessions. All of them ended in substantial gains for the plebeians.[3] None the less they were seditions, openly setting at nought magisterial authority and dignity. To provide the participants, and above all the leaders, with a fully effective safeguard against punishment it was held necessary to grant amnesty by legislative or quasi-legislative action. True, we are told so only with regard to three of the five cases, the first, the second and the fourth.[4] But what we hear about the remaining two is so brief and vague that silence on this point means nothing.

Dionysius' stand in this matter is very special. In his narrative of the first secession, the topic of amnesty is prominent.[5] However, according to him, the plebeians, when offered this boon, replied that, having done no wrong, they did not need it:

---

[1] Livy 7.41.3: *ne quis eam rem ioco seriove cuiquam exprobraret.*
[2] Such as a prohibition of lending on interest: Livy 7.42.1f.
[3] 494 BC, institution of the tribunate; 449 BC, removal of the decemvirs and improvements in the status of the plebeians; 445 BC, further improvements and admission of intermarriage between the orders; 342 BC, abolition of political and economic grievances; 287 BC, recognition of plebiscites as binding on both orders.
[4] First secession of 494: Livy 7.41.2. Here, in support of an amnesty for the secession of 342, the enactment of such a measure following the two earlier secessions of 494 and 449 is pleaded. In his discussion of the first secession itself, Livy omits the amnesty: he is altogether extremely short as to arrangements once the plebeians had agreed to return—2.32.1ff. On the amnesty question in Dionysius' account of the first secession I shall comment presently in the text. Second secession of 449: Livy 3.53.4, 54.5. Dionysius' work shows a gap at this juncture, *i.e.*, after 11.44.5. Fourth secession of 342 BC: Livy 7.41.2f.
[5] 6.47.2 at the end, 48.1f., 71.2, 72.5, 77.3. In conformity with his general picture of the constitutional set-up, it would be granted by the senate.

148

on the contrary, it was the patricians who needed it—their wrongdoing had produced the present condition.

The view of causation and culpability underlying this approach has a long history, involving such concepts as *archon cheiron adikon*, 'he who starts with wrongful hands':[1] I cannot here enter into it. What I would call attention to is a strand in the conservative philosophy which may be summed up by *noblesse oblige*.[2] Dionysius, while firmly on the side of the haves, is a determined opponent of cruel and tyrannical treatment of the have-nots. Up to a point, the secessionists of 494 BC do enjoy his sympathies. A master, if he is to be secure in his power, must not abuse his subjects; indeed, so long as they are compliant—Uncle Toms—he may be genuinely fond of them; he has every reason to be. This goes also for Livy; and the idea that responsibility for a sedition may lie with those against whom it is directed rather than those who actually undertake it occurs in his work too, in connection with the second secession.[3] Apparently, it was widely accepted in Roman historical tradition, though the inference that the revolutionaries could do without an amnesty is met only in Dionysius.

How the dilemma was in the end resolved, he does not inform us. I guess the tradition that an amnesty was granted was too definite for him to contradict it. On the other hand, as he approved of the argument that in the circumstances the measure made no sense, he did not want to admit that it was passed after all. To say nothing was his way out. Unfortunately, whatever he may have written about this subject in his story of the second secession is lost, owing to a gap in his treatise as it has come down to us.[4]

Perhaps I should add that both Livy and Dionysius have it that, after the overthrow of the decemvirs as a result of the second secession, some of the most hated aristocrats were prosecuted for specific crimes—like arbitrary enslavement or scourging of a citizen—which the despotic regime had enabled them

---

[1] *E.g.*, Xenophon, *Cyropaedia* 1.5.13. Cp. my brother's remarks in Benjamin Daube, *Zu den Rechtsproblemen in Aischylos' Agamemnon*, 1938, pp. 76f., 80f., 83, 87, 137.
[2] The author of this maxim is Pierre-Marc-Gaston duc de Lévis (see Büchmann, *Geflügelte Worte*, 26th ed. by Krieger, 1920, p. 290). He published his work in 1808, by which time he had spent several years in England. He may well have profited by the political wisdom of his hosts.
[3] 3.50.14: *quippe ab ipsis datum locum seditioni esse.*   [4] After 11.44.5.

to commit; and they were executed, driven to suicide or exiled. When this had gone on for a while, a reaction in the public mood set in—as is bound to happen in such situations unless the social system has really undergone a radical change. It was the plebeian tribunes who vetoed further arraignments.[1]

---

[1] Livy 3.59.2f. Dionysius 11.46.5 speaks of an amnesty at the instance of the tribunes. Whether he is thinking of a more formal decree than Livy must be left open.

INDEX

Esther, Book of—*contd.*
  resistance in, 14–16, 87–91
  role of women in, 15
  types of women in, 15–16, 88–9
Euripides
  impiety charge, 72
  on self-extinction, 96–7
  version of Antigone, 40
Euthyphro, 74n
evasion
  in Esther, 112
  of Peter, 113–14
  of rules in modern society, 10
  on question of Jewishness, 112,
    113
Exodus story
  absence of illegality, 126
  desire for liberation, 125
  God as the liberator, 125, 126–7
  Hebrews as the majority people,
    124
  oppression, 124, 125
  question of guilt, 127–8
  role of Moses, 125–6, 127
  slaying of the firstborn, 127
Exodus, Book of, majority ruling,
    81
extinction of minorities
  as gesture of defiance, 92
  attitudes of women and
    children, 96
  God's view of, 95–6
  Heracles on, 96–7
  Josephus on, 92
  justification for, 94–5
  Livy on, 92
  Polybius on, 92
  threat of mass, 98–100
  voluntary, 92–7
extradition
  decision of secret synod on,
    99–100
  for crime, 100
  of named person, 99–100
  of Saul's sons, 12
  of Sicarii, 96, 101
  of unnamed person, 99
  refusal to extradite, 98–9
  threat of penalties on failure to,
    98–9
eye for an eye, 109–10

fable(s)
  ancient writers of, 53
  cultural levels and, 54, 130–1
  of ant and cicada, 135
  of ass changing masters, 125,
    132
  of ass indifferent to masters,
    54–5, 125, 132
  of eyes and mouth, 133
  of fox and crow, 135
  of legs and stomach, 138
  of Menenius, 130–1, 132–3
  of stomach and head, 138
  popularity of, among plebeians,
    130–1
  popularity of, among slaves,
    130–1
  simplicity of, 54, 131
  use by Phaedrus, 54–5
  use of, by slaves and freedmen,
    53–4, 71
    see also Aesop, Menenius,
      Phaedrus
faithfulness
  in apocalyptic literature, 86, 87
  of women, 33
Fall, the, 61, 62
families, family
  fragmented into sects, 46–7
  idolatry among, 45–6
  Jesus' refusal to recognise, 46
  natural, 47
  true, 47
father(s)
  Deuteronomic code addressed
    to, 46
  disobedience of daughters,
    38–9
  filial independence, 49
fiction, interaction of life and, 40
filibuster
  as para-civil disobedience, x
  gadflies and, 73
  use of word, xn
Flavius, Cnaeus, 119–22
Florus, 143
followers, master's responsibility
    for, 74
force
  justification for use of, 2
  replaced by persuasion, 64

Ibsen, *The Doll's House*, 1–2, 6
idolatry
  denial of Jewishness and,
    112–13
  enticement to, 45–6
  penalty for, 52
  prohibition of, in Jewish law,
    83, 95, 97, 112
  refrain from, in Daniel, 83, 84
  view that idolators are not
    religious community, 81–2
independence
  movements within the law,
    123–4
  of India, 123
  of Southern Rhodesia, 123–4
  of the Hebrews, 124–8
  of the Northern kingdom,
    128–9
  violence and, 123–4
India, independence of, 123
inheritance
  Jewish law of, 49
  Roman law of, 52
Iphigeneia, 36
Irvine, burning of bank at, 104
Isaac
  Jacob and Esau, 49–50
  sacrifice of, 36
Isaiah, 105
Ishmael, Rabbi, 42
Israel, absence of death penalty,
  100

Jabneh, Jews of
  Agrippa's letter, 93, 94, 95
  God as the higher authority,
    95–6
  Josephus' accounts of, 94
  Philo's account, 92–7
Jacob
  as a prophet, 63
  blessing of, 49–50
  daughter of, 45
Jason, 34–5
Jehoiakim, King, 69–70, 72
Jehu, 65
Jeremiah
  and the burning of the books,
    69, 72
  Cassandra and, 69

imprisonment of, 67–8
in hiding, 70
obstructionism of, 65
peaceful symbolism, 105
personal courage of, 70
question of escape, 68
remonstrance on use of temple,
  106, 107
Jeremiah, Rabbi, ix–x
Jeroboam, 128–9
Jesus
  arrest of 110–12: absence of
    objection to violence,
    111–12; as insult, 110, 112;
    as resistance, 111, 112
  burial of, 12–13
  Cleansing of the Temple,
    101–8, 112: pacifist view of,
    102–3, 109; prophetic
    symbolism, 103–5; reasons
    for violent behaviour, 106–8;
    use of violence, 101–2, 103
  contrasting views on death of,
    100–1
  discourse with rabbis, 49
  disobedience from religious
    conviction, 46
  obedience to God, 47–8
  refusal to recognise parents, 46
  responsibility for followers, 74
  retreat of, 70
  Sermon on the Mount, 109–10
  staying behind at the temple,
    47–9
  submission to parents, 48–9
  suggested insanity, 46
Jews, Jewish
  age of majority, 47
  ethics and tyranny, 9–10
  minority in the Book of Esther,
    87–91
  monarchy and the prophets,
    63–5
  remarriage customs, 13–14
  rising of 117AD, 131–2
  survival for cause, 79
  view of heroism, 79
Jewishness
  disavowal of: private, 112, 113,
    114; public, 112, 113
  equivocation on, 112–13

violence—*contd.*
    of groups under coercion, 34
    of prophets, 64, 105
    of slaves, 52
    of youth, 43
    sedition and, 102
    threat of, xi
    transition to, 102
    withholding of, regarded as a
        favour, 131–2
Volscians, 142

war
    anti-war play of Aristophanes,
        117–19
    as a diversion, 142
    as a unifier, 142
    defection to the enemy, 142–4
    effect on women, 17
    first plebeian secession during,
        130, 133, 139
    leading to disunity, 142–3
    liberation through, 142–3
    love and, 17
    military interpretation of fables,
        138–9
    opportunities for secession,
        124–5, 129
    opportunities for supression,
        124–5
    Plato on causes of, 18
    plebeians evading levy, 142
    refusing to fight, 142
    resistance to, 17
    women's efforts to stop, 18
War Scroll, 87
weak, supported by the strong,
    37, 38
West, Mae, 37
William II, Emperor, 133–4
wisdom
    centres of young, 42–3
    in the Book of Esther, 88
    old age and, 41–2, 52
witch of Endor, 69
withdrawal
    in Menenius' fable, 130
    of plebeians, 130, 143
    see also secession
women
    advocates, 25–6

appeal to love, 39, 52
appropriateness of non-
    violence to, 6
as outside the power structure,
    5–6
assimilation of men's set of
    values, 23–7
defencelessness of, 37–8
fighting for men, 18
government of, 21
in the Book of Esther, 15–16,
    88–9
men fighting for, 18
of Greece, 1–22
of Rome, 23–40
of the Bible, 1–22
personal view of life, 6, 21, 22
question of definition, 1
rights, in Jewish society, 13–14
rights, in *Lysistrata*, 18–19
Women's Liberation, 18, 27

Xenophon, 3, 134–5
Xerxes, 91

youth
    advice to Rehoboam by, 128
    bettering of status, 49–50
    corruption of, 74–5
    differing views on possession
        and position, 43–5
    disobedience, causes of, 43–52
    following a new messianic
        creed, 47–8
    generosity of, 44–5
    in the Bible, 41–2
    mastery of new circumstances,
        43
    old age and, 41–3, 51–2
    permitted civil disobedience of,
        45–6
    religion, 45–6
    sense of honour, 45
    sense of national mission, 43
    teachers giving prominence to,
        43
    traditional obedience to old,
        48

Zealots, 87
Zeus, 60